The Presence of the Past

A.M.D.G.

The Presence of the Past

Christian Heritage Sites in the Rhins of Galloway

JOHN McLEAN

With sketches and maps by the author

JOHN DONALD PUBLISHERS LTD
EDINBURGH

ISBN 0 85976 474 5

British Library Cataloguing in Publication Data

A catalogue record for this book is available
from the British Library.

PostScript Typesetting & Origination by Brinnoven, Livingston.
Printed & bound in Great Britain by Bell & Bain Ltd, Glasgow.

Contents

Note on References

To avoid cumbersome citations in the text, references appear as abbreviations within parentheses. For example, (Q1, 86) indicates page 86 of Reference No. Q1 (an article in *The Innes Review*) cited in full in the reference list on page 178 of this volume.

Introduction

Christianity is an integral part of life in Scotland today. But that Christianity had a beginning. It began in Galloway, in south-west Scotland. Church life and organisation took root with St Ninian, who established the first stone church in Scotland at Whithorn. This event, by tradition, is said to have taken place in AD 397. Within Ninian's lifetime that root grew, with shoots providing other centres of Christianity.

Whithorn is in the Machars area, the eastern half of Wigtownshire.

The Rhins and adjoining land, up to the area of Glenluce, make up the western half of Wigtownshire.

Within Ninian's lifetime Christianity was brought in an organised form to the Rhins. It grew. And the heritage stemming from that growth is so rich, and yet so little known.

What follows is an attempt to record that Christian heritage in a systematic way, showing how the Church became etablished throughout the Rhins from the 5th to the 16th century. This was a long period of growth and consolidation. It was also a period marked by an infusion of diverse peoples and cultures. This has largely served to enrich and colour that which has come down to us as our Christian heritage.

Elsewhere, the ensuing centuries are well documented and historical records are available to trace the way Christianity has continued in the Rhins up to the present day.

A church building is a silent witness. The people associated with it are its living witnesses. They really express the faith that the building represents. These are the 'living stones' that St Peter (1 Peter 2:5) speaks of. In this way, the church buildings themselves have a sacramental quality — they are a visible sign of the reality of faith.

So it is with our ancient church buildings, their remains, their sites. They are a chronicle, an historic record; they give us their silent witness of the texture of our Christian heritage.

By the middle of the 16th century the Rhins and its adjacent area contained two abbeys, eight other parish churches, and as many as another thirty-four chapels. This richness and concentration of so many religious buildings makes the area an eminently important centre of early and medieval Christianity. To find so many churches and chapels compactly situated is very remarkable. Each one has a story to tell. None has survived intact. Some have disappeared, or nearly so; and some have ruins that remain. Very few of the latter are carefully looked after; most of them, sadly, are neglected.

We owe it to our past not to neglect them. We owe it to our present age to make them better known and appreciated. And we owe it to our future inheritors to preserve and maintain that which remains. Our heritage is too precious to do less than that. By not disregarding our past we become more aware of our own identity, and this interplay prompts us to pass on the mantle and the spirit of our Christian heritage to the generations ahead.

This book is dedicated to that.

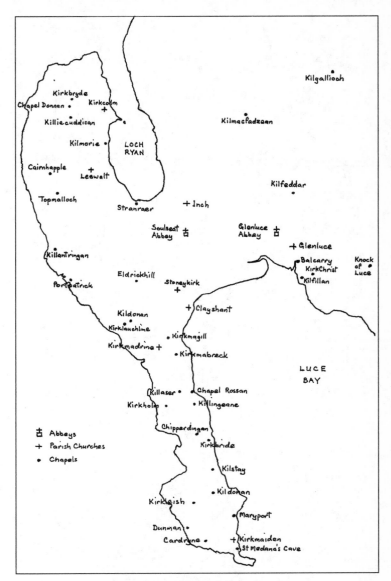

Map 1. Christian Heritage Sites

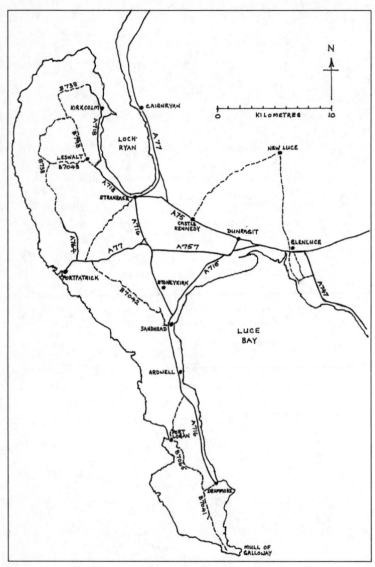

Map 2. Routes in the Rhins

Location of the Rhins

The Rhins is a land area consisting of two joined peninsulas, situated in the south-west corner of Scotland. It lies in Wigtownshire, within the more general area known as Galloway. To the west of the Rhins there is the North Channel of the Irish Sea, and to the east there are two sea lochs: Loch Ryan opening to the north, and Luce Bay to the south. The rolling countryside stretches some 46 kilometres (29 miles) north to south, and up to about 8 kilometres (5 miles) east to west. On the whole it is thinly populated, with a sprinkling of farms and villages, and one larger seaport town, Stranraer.

The coast of Northern Ireland is only about 35 kilometres (22 miles) from the nearest point of contact with the Rhins of Galloway. Over the centuries this nearness has made it a commonly-used sea crossing between Scotland and Ireland. Centuries ago, many small inlets would have provided landings for smaller boats. Nowadays, apart from a number of harbour anchorages for small boats, the main sea ferries operate from Stranraer and Cairnryan.

The title 'Rhins' may have been given to this area of Galloway either in Celtic or Roman times. The Gaelic *rinn* or *roinn* means a peninsula or point. The Latin language used by the Romans included some adopted Greek words. In Greek, *rhis rhinos* means nose. If the Romans gave this descriptive name to the area first, then the Gaelic-speaking Celtic people may have used and adapted this. The title has come down to us today as Rhins, and describes the double promontory in this south-western part of Scotland.

In what follows, the Rhins will be combined with its associated area of West Wigtownshire up to and including the area of Glenluce. The latter northerly part of the county is known as the Moors.

Centuries of People

For at least nine thousand years there has been a long process of assimilation, by which various groups of people have come to and settled in the Galloway area. Their languages and their cultures have been absorbed. Some have had lasting influences, others just for a time.

The first humans seem to have reached Scotland from the south about 7000 BC. They were few in number and of a semi-nomadic type.

Neolithic settlers arrived in Scotland from about 4000 BC. In Galloway, evidence of their presence is provided by a number of chambered tombs, usually built on a hillside and each apparently providing some sort of religious focus or shrine, perhaps associated with ancestor worship.

Stone ceremonial circles, dating from the 3rd and 2nd millenia BC, are evidence of religious and social development in the Galloway area.

Standing stones, in ones, twos or threes, mark Bronze Age burials or denote boundaries or meeting places.

Archaeological evidence shows that between 1000 BC and AD 400 people in this part of Scotland lived in crannogs, hill forts and brochs.

When the Romans established themselves in south-west Scotland, about AD 80, they recorded three distinct tribal groups — the Damnonii (of Ayrshire), the Selgovae (of Dumfries and the Borders area) and the Novantae (of Galloway).

After AD 400 there was a Roman withdrawal. At this time, over a wider area, there had emerged from the various tribal groupings four distinct kingdoms — the Celtic Britons of Strathclyde, the Irish Scots of Dalriada, the Germanic Angles of Northumbria, and the Picts of the North and East of Scotland.

In the period between the 6th and 9th centuries there was a substantial Celtic, Gaelic-speaking settlement in Galloway, which was very Church-orientated.

Throughout the 8th century, Galloway was under Northumbrian Anglian rule. Then, from about AD 800, Viking raids and settlement of the Norsemen broke the Anglian domination.

There followed a second main Gaelic settlement in Galloway, that of the *Gall-ghaidhil* 'foreign Norse Gael'. It is from this group of people that Galloway derives its name. Existent local communities were won or forced over to the Norse way of life. Similar communities came from the Hebrides and Ireland. Though subjected to Scandinavian influences, the people of the Gall-ghaidhil period retained their Gaelic language.

In the ensuing period of the 12th and early 13th centuries, the Gall-ghaidhil of Galloway had its own territorial lordship. But generally the Scots became the dominant group and established a single kingdom, advancing their hold on all the rest of what was then called Scotland.

At this 12th century period it would seem that not one cultural group was dominant in Galloway. There was a complex of ethnic groups with different languages: Anglo-Saxon, English, Gaelic, Norse and Church Latin. Clerical writings of the 13th century refer to the English, Scots and Gallovidians, indicating that the latter polyglot society was considered distinct from the remainder of Scotland.

Following the conquest of England by the Normans, their influence filtered into Scotland. From about AD 1100 a feudal system was instituted, but Norse/Celtic elites were still in Wigtownshire into the 14th century.

The next major influx to the population started in the early 19th century, with a growing number of poverty-stricken Irish immigrants. In mid-century, with the potato crop failure in Ireland, Galloway received and absorbed an increased number of these Irish immigrants.

Out of all this historical development Galloway, including the Rhins, has assimilated influences from Celts, Romans, Angles, Gaels, Vikings, Normans and, latterly, the Irish. Language, speech, customs, traditions, culture have all been affected. This is all part of the assimilated character of today's Gallovidians.

But an essential part of this story is the influnce that religion has had upon the people of the area, through the centuries and up to today. Religious influence is an integral part of heritage. It is important to look at this now in a more detailed way.

Christianity

Beginnings

Pre-Christian religion is strongly evidenced in the Galloway region of Scotland by the surviving chambered cairns, stone circles, standing stones and ancient cists. Added to this are remaining names of places and sites alluding to druidical times. Spirituality seems to have played an integral part in people's lives in the past.

It is not easy to define the interface of superstition and faith. Primitive faith may be judged to have been much infused with superstition — yet it reflects a human aspiration for contact, for harmony, for favour, for good relationship with a power and a reality beyond, yet touching, human life.

Christians believe this and more. They believe in a perfect God, a loving God, a just, forgiving, providential, all-powerful, creating, revealing God. A God who, at the wisest time, manifested himself to us in all the vulnerability of a human baby. This human-divine person, Jesus Christ, grew to manhood and revealed his divine power, plan and provision, that would so benefit us.

In Jesus, the unutterable is uttered. The mystery of God is expressed in a single, perfect, complete word. As St John says at the beginning of his Gospel: 'The Word was made flesh, he lived among us, and we saw his glory.' (John, 1:14).

Christians believe that God shared our humanity in the person of Jesus. God intervened in this personal way to restore our humanity, the nature and destiny of which were thwarted by the wilful misuse of our God-given freedom. Our Lord gave his life to redeem us. He rose from the dead, and invites us to share in the mystery and reality of his Resurrection and Ascension into heaven. He invites us to share in his kingdom forever, and to bring its reality into our everyday lives, wherever we are and throughout the world.

Our Lord lived and died in the Holy Land. He preached, taught, performed good works, and showed his divine power by many miracles. He is not only an exemplar for his followers, but a unifying, vivifying and sanctifying mystery into which his followers centre their lives in his. He prepared for his continuing presence in human life and history by instituting a church.

You are Peter and on this rock I will build my Church. And the gates of the underworld can never hold out against it. I will give you the keys of the kingdom of heaven: whatever you bind on earth shall be considered bound in heaven; whatever you loose on earth shall be considered loosed in heaven. (Matthew 16:18-19).

St Peter was the leader of the apostles, the twelve men specially chosen by Our Lord. It was during Our Lord's public ministry, the last three years of his life, that he called these special followers to share his life and work. He trained them to continue this after his death, resurrection and ascension into heaven. He promised them the presence of the Holy Spirit to lead them to the complete truth (John 16:13), and to inspire them to carry out the Church work entrusted to them. Thus his kingdom was to be extended in time and history.

At the time of Our Lord's life on earth, Europe, the Middle East and North Africa were all under the dominance of the Roman Empire. The apostles effectively built up the infant Church, despite secular and religious opposition. St Peter's apostolic work took him to the heart of the Roman Empire, to Rome, where he exercised his bishop's ministry. Both he and St Paul were martyred there for their Faith. Earlier, Our Lord's crucifixion had not stemmed the birth of the Church. The martyrdom of the apostles, likewise, did not eliminate the rooting, development and continuity of the Church. Linus, Cletus, Clement, and a line of others, followed in succession to St Peter as bishops of Rome and papal leaders of the Church.

Surviving letters of St Ignatius, bishop of Antioch, who was martyred at Rome in AD *c.* 107, speak of the threefold ministry of bishop, priest and deacon as an already-established feature of Church life.

The first three centuries of Church growth was under the shadow of the pagan Roman Empire and marked by periods of persecution. Still the Church grew. This was also a period of reflection and refinement of truth, made necessary by a succession of heretical beliefs. The infant Church was coming of age.

In the year 313, Constantine, the Roman emperor, issued a decree, the Edict of Milan, which emancipated Christians, allowing them to hold property and worship publicly. Such freedom saw a burgeoning of Christian life and activity. Churches could then be built. Constantine himself arranged for the erection of the first Basilica of St Peter, in Rome, at the burial site of the saint. He also arranged for the building of other Roman basilicas, including that of St Paul's outside-the-walls.

To Pope Miltiades and his successors the Emperor Constantine gave the Lateran palace, which became the papal residence and the centre of administration for the Roman Catholic Church. This basilica became, and remains to this day, the cathedral of Rome. On its façade is the inscription, 'The Mother and Head of all churches of the City and of the World'. From the 14th century the Vatican became the residence of the Popes.

During the 4th century two major Councils of the Church were held: one in 325, at Nicaea; and another, in 381, at Constantinople. Out of these came the Nicene Creed, a Church-approved encapsulation of essential elements of the Catholic Faith.

St Ninian

Into this 4th century of Church emancipation, consolidation and growth, there comes a man who will have a profound influence in Galloway and Scotland.

The earliest written account of St Ninian comes from the 7th century saint, the Venerable Bede. In his *Ecclesiastical History*, written at Wearmouth, Jarrow, he records:

> The southern Picts who dwell on this side of those mountains had, it is reported, long before forsaken the errors of paganism and embraced the truth by the preaching of Ninias, a most reverend bishop and holy man of the British nation, who had been regularly instructed at Rome in the faith and mysteries of the truth. His episcopal see, named after St Martin the Bishop and famous for a church in his honour (wherein Ninias himself and many other saints rest in the body), is now in the possession of the English nation. The place belongs to the province of the Bernicians and is commonly called the White House, because he there built a church of stone, which was not usual amongst the Britons.

Ninian was probably a Cumbrian Briton. He seems to have grown up in the Solway area. At this time, accepting Ninian's birth to have been in the second half of the 4th century, the Romans had been established in the country for over three centuries. Although the people generally were pagan, Christianity would have reached the area, if only through contact with Christians of the occupying Roman power, which by now was tolerant of Christianity. In England, the Church was sufficiently established for three British bishops to be present at the Council of Arles in the year 314 (P1,3). In Scotland, the ground was ready, the seed was sown, the cultivator was about to be sent for the harvest. God's choice was Ninian. He had gone to Rome.

He experienced the Christian renaissance of the 4th century, the church building, the more visible organisation of the Church, the consolidation and expression of the unity of the Faith in the promulgated Creed, and the developing liturgical life of the Christian community. This was the period of St Ambrose and St Augustine. Ninian would benefit from the learning and the stimulation of the Church life he experienced during his time, probably years, in Rome. He was ordained as a bishop and returned home. On his journey he would be likely to travel through France. At this time St Martin of Tours was a prominent churchman. Whether by meeting him or by learning of his reputation, Ninian evidently was impressed by this holy bishop.

St Ninian arrived back in his native land at a period nearing the end or at the end of the Roman occupation. He established himself in south-west Scotland, in Galloway, and set up his see at Whithorn. It was there that he had the first stone church built in Scotland, which was dedicated to St Martin. St Martin died in November 397, the year when it is said that Ninian built his Whithorn church, according to the account given in the *Life of St Ninian* by St Aelred, abbot of Rievaulx Abbey, in the 12th century. Modern scholars vary in their dating of St Ninian at Whithorn, but his period there stretched into the 5th century.

Though dedicated to St Martin, Ninian's church was more generally referred to as *Candida Casa*, the White House, from which comes the place name Whithorn.

> An existing Christian community may have existed at this site before the arrival, as its bishop, of Ninian. His first stone church does not appear to have been monastic but had apparently become such by the 8th century, the change perhaps stemming from the activities of Irish Christian monks in the late 6th century. (B, 103)

The above later-monastic view by Cowan (1976) contrasts with the early-monastic view expressed by Brooke (1994). The latter, from the findings of recent excavations at Whithorn, indicating a 5th century monastic settlement, contends that like St Martin, who was both bishop and monk, St Ninian too combined these two offices.

Ninian's work flourished, his community grew; he and his missionary co-workers seem to have achieved the conversion of the southern Picts within a lifetime. His influence seems to have extended to Ireland too. Part of the consolidation of such gains for the Church would be Ninian's ordination of priests to minister and spiritually care for such an expanded Christian community.

Through the foundation at Whithorn, St Ninian's effect on Celtic Chrisianity was considerable, but his success among the Picts seems to have been rather short-lived: St Patrick (*c*. 389-*c*. 461), in his letter to Coroticus, refers to them as apostates. But he had paved the way for St Columba and St Kentigern. (J, III, 569)

MacQueen (Q2, 17ff) writes:

Ninian himself had contacts of some kind with Ireland, and, although doubts have been cast on some of the evidence, in the period between 450 and 650, Candida Casa would seem to have been in close touch with developments in the Irish church. Partly as a consequence, some Gaelic speakers settled in Galloway during this period.

If, as St Patrick indicates in his letter to Coroticus, the southern Scottish Picts did not hold on to the Faith brought to them by Ninian, there is yet ample evidence, through the survival of the see of Whithorn and the establishment of other dioceses, churches and monasteries, that periodic setbacks did not prevent the ensuing general spread and growth of the institutional Church throughout Scotland.

The Catholic Centuries

During the early centuries of the Church, monasticism had developed out of the root provided by St Antony (251-356) in Egypt, and refined later by St Benedict (died *c*. 547) in Italy.

In Scotland, two saints were to take up the mantle of Christian leadership in the 6th century Church.

St Kentigern (or Mungo) (518-603), born in Scotland, established himself and a community at Glasgow, where he later became its first bishop. For a short time he had his see at Hoddam, in Dumfriesshire.

A contemporary saint, Columba (*c*. 521-597), came from Ireland in the year 563 and settled, with twelve companions, on the island of Iona. From his monastery there he and his fellow monks set about the conversion of the Picts in the Highlands of Scotland. After Columba's death, his influence lasted on and dominated the churches of Scotland, Ireland and Northumbria. For three-quarters of a century and more, Celtic Christians in those lands upheld Columban traditions in certain matters of order and ritual, in opposition to those of Rome itself.

Throughout these centuries, Scottish Church affairs were affected by historical events within the country and by events beyond the country.

Pope Gregory the Great, who died in 604, was the first pope who had been a monk. He was a great reformer and consolidator of the Church. In 596 he sent St Augustine to England. As Archbishop of

Canterbury, where he established his see, Augustine worked for the conversion of the country and the restoration and development of the Church.

In 634, St Aidan, an Irish-born monk from Iona, was made Bishop of Northumbria. He established his see and a monastery at Lindisfarne, the Holy Isle. Thus Celtic Christianity spread from Scotland to the North of England.

From the late 6th to the 8th century Celtic monks seem to have extended their influence into Galloway.

St Cuthbert (*c.* 636-687) was a monk at Melrose before transferring to Lindisfarne, in Northumbria. His holy life combined monasticism, apostolic labour and solitude as a hermit. He travelled, and was widely known and loved in both England and Scotland. He visited Galloway. The town of Kirkcudbright is named after him, as is the county. He was persuaded and was consecrated Bishop of Lindisfarne in York Minster on Easter day 685 by St Theodore, Archbishop of Canterbury. St Cuthbert's diocese extended over Northumbria and Cumbria.

During this time, in the year 664, a great synod of the Church took place at Whitby Abbey. This was to decide on what day Easter should be observed and to resolve vexed questions between Roman and Celtic observances. The outcome was that Roman customs were to prevail over the Celtic ones in England. Throughout the ensuing centuries this would influence the Church in Scotland. It was not until the medieval period that the Celtic Culdee traditions were replaced in Scotland. This was in no small part due to the rapid expansion, from the beginning of the 12th century, of so many new foundations of the Church's traditional and emerging monastic and religious Orders.

So from 397, Candida Casa, St Ninian's foundation at Whithorn, exerted a continued influence, attracting religious-minded visitors from Ireland. Irish-speaking farmers and fishermen increasingly established themselves in Galloway. Iona (563) and Lindisfarne (634) were responsible for missionary work extending to the Galloway area. In the period, therefore, between the 6th and 9th centuries there was a substantial Celtic, Gaelic-speaking settlement in Galloway, which was Christian and under Church influence. Many of the church foundations in the area are of Celtic origin and date from this period. (Q2, 24-6)

At Whithorn a succession of Northumbrian bishops commenced about 725. This succession ended with Bishop Badulf, who took office in 790. From *c.* 833 the bishopric at Whithorn appears to have lapsed for three centuries.

This was a period marked by Scandinavian invasions. In 687, York fell to the Danes. Norsemen made incursions into various parts of England and Scotland. At the end of the 9th century the Lindisfarne community found temporary shelter at Whithorn. (Q1, 86)

The Danish conquest of York may actually have stimulated ties with Whithorn, as Scandinavian colonisation of north-western England and southern Dumfriesshire preserved a corridor of contact from Yorkshire to the Solway. (Q1, 86)

From the end of the 9th, through the 10th, and into the 11th centuries, there followed a second main Gaelic settlement in Galloway, that of the *Gall-ghaidhil* ('foreign, Norse, Gael'). These were people who had forsaken their Christian baptism, having been influenced by incoming Viking-Norsemen. This group consisted of existing Irish settlers won or forced over to the Norse way of life, as well as similarly-influenced groups who had migrated from Ireland and the Hebrides. Despite their association with Norsemen, the *Gall-ghaidhil* people were primarily speakers of Gaelic rather than a Scandinavian language (Q2, 27). But the influence of this period is evident in the substitution of the Norse *Kirk* for the Gaelic *Kil* (*Cille*) in church titles. At worst, the Gall-ghaidhill engaged in violation of churches and sacrament; at best, they had a compromised disaffection for or toleration of the Church. By the end of the 11th century there was a greater degree of toleration, even support for the Church, and it may be then that Iona's influence again came to the fore, possibly leading at that time to the founding of some further Gallovidian churches, with dedications to earlier saints associated with Iona and Ireland.

> In the 12th and early 13th centuries the Gall-ghaidhil existed as a virtually independent state with their own laws and customs administered by rulers (titled, Lord of Galloway) whom the Irish annalists habitually describe as kings — Fergus, who died in 1161 and his descendent rulers down to just after 1234 to three daughters of Alan, each of whom married a Norman: Helen, wife of Roger de Quincy, Derbforgaill (Dervorgilla), wife of John de Balliol, and Christina, wife of William de Fortibus. Derbforgaill inherited the modern Kirkcudbright, founded Sweetheart Abbey and endowed Balliol College, Oxford, in memory of her husband. (Q2, 27-8)

To the Celtic, Anglo-Saxon and Scandinavian influences came the Normans, who were to put their character on the fabric of society and be influential too in the life of the Church, first in England, then in Scotland.

In 1066, William the Conqueror and his Norman supporters took over Anglo-Saxon England. The might involved contrasts with the gentleness with which Scotland was conquered. This came about by the fleeing from the invading Normans of the courtly Margaret d'Outremer, an Anglo-Saxon kinswoman of Edward the Confessor. She was given refuge in Scotland, and in 1070 married King Malcolm Canmore. Margaret's personal saintliness, grace and education influenced King and country, leading to a renaissance in courtly, country and Church life. Three of her sons became kings, most notably David 1 (*c*. 1080-1153). He consolidated the reforming work in the country, started by his saintly mother. By this time Norman barons in England had endowed the building of a series of new monasteries. David extended this by inviting new religious foundations in Scotland. Besides establishing five northern dioceses, it was during his reign, when Fergus was Lord of Galloway, that Bishop Gilla-Aldan was installed at Whithorn in *c*. 1128, restoring this see, which seems to have lapsed from *c*. 833. This appointment was recognised as under the metropolitan authority of York, and remained so until 1355.

David 1 founded numerous monasteries, including Cistercian ones at Melrose and Dundrennan. It was from these that Glenluce Abbey was founded in 1192 by Roland, Lord of Galloway.

Soulseat Abbey, in the Rhins, was a 12th-century foundation of the Premonstratensian Order.

Despite ravages brought about because of wars between Scotland and England during the medieval centuries, monastic, conventual and diocesan Church life continued to be an integral part of the national life, providing spiritual and temporal care and expertise. Robert the Bruce and John Baliol and a line of royal patrons played their varied parts.

The Church was the main provider of available education. Approved by papal bulls, universities were instituted by Scottish bishops at St Andrews (1413), Glasgow (1451) and Aberdeen (1495).

With papal approval, the See of Whithorn became a suffragan of St Andrews in 1472, and then of Glasgow in 1492.

Throughout the medieval period diocesan parish churches had been largely annexed and appropriated to the monasteries. This meant that some or all of the parish revenues (tiends) went to the monasteries, and the monasteries supplied the parishes with religious or secular priest-vicars. Towards the period of the Reformation, lay-commendators were being appointed to lordship of the abbeys, exercising secular control of the abbeys' revenues and property.

Of these times MacQueen (Q2, 31) writes:

> It is clear that for most people in Galloway life continued to be a matter primarily of agriculture and stock-rearing, with attendance on Sundays and feast-days at the local church, which was probably administered by a vicar appointed from one of the monasteries which had gained control over most of the parishes.

There were peaks and troughs in the life of the Church, and, as always, there were saints and sinners. By the mid-16th century the spiritual life of the Church was quite compromised by secularity. Reform was imminent.

The Reformation in Scotland

Throughout 16th-century Europe, saints of the calibre of Teresa of Avila, John of the Cross, Ignatius of Loyola, Robert Bellarmine, Peter Canisius, Charles Borromeo, Philip Neri, Cajetan and Angela Merici worked for reformation within the Catholic Church. On the Continent, Martin Luther, John Calvin, Huldreich Zwingli, Martin Bucer and, in Scotland, John Knox, Patrick Hamilton, George Wishart and others promoted reform leading to severance from the Catholic Church.

Profound reform was set in place within the Catholic Church by the Council of Trent, convened in 1545 and concluded in 1563.

By this time some reformers had abandoned allegiance to the Catholic Church and instituted various opposing forms of faith-life, worship and church community.

In 1534, King Henry VIII had assumed the headship of the Church in England.

In Scotland, Protestantism, led by John Knox and others, overthrew the existing Catholicism, which had been weakened by secularisation and politics. In 1560, Catholic traditions going back to St Ninian in the 4th century were rejected by an Act of the Scottish Parliament. This Act abolished papal spiritual jurisdiction in Scotland, banned the celebration of the Mass, and accepted the Confession of Faith, composed by John Knox and his fellow-leaders, which described the Roman Catholic Church as 'the horrible harlot, the kirk malignant'. Church lands were appropriated largely by the nobles and church buildings were taken over by the reformers. Monastic and other religious communities were either unable to continue or allowed to wither away.

While the reformed Presbyterian Church in Scotland consolidated its position and grew, Catholicism, although officially suppressed, was not entirely extinguished. During the penal times, for just over two centuries following the Reformation of 1560, there were remoter parts of the country which remained Catholic. Despite difficulties, there were also a few prominent families who retained the Catholic Faith. To serve such remaining Catholics there was a slender supply of missionary priests. These were mainly young men who had gone to the Continent, and having been educated, trained and ordained as priests, then returned to Scotland, despite the difficulties, to minister to the remaining Catholics.

In 1690, further penal laws against Catholic education were introduced.

With the passage of time, attitudes began to change. With such toleration, in 1793, the penal law against the celebration of Mass was repealed. From that time, Catholic churches started to be built again. In 1829 there was a further penal law repeal, restoring freedoms and franchise to Catholics.

Throughout the 19th century, the Catholic population of Scotland was expanded by the influx of poor and hungry Irish immigrants, exacerbated by the Irish Famine, which was at its peak from 1845 to 1847. Many new Catholic parishes were set up to minister to their needs.

In 1878, the Scottish Catholic hierarchy was restored, with two archdioceses, Glasgow and St Andrews & Edinburgh, and four dioceses, Aberdeen, Argyll & The Isles, Dunkeld and Galloway. (In 1947, two further dioceses were erected, Motherwell and Paisley.)

In 1878, Bishop John McLachlan resumed the see of Galloway. The present bishop, Maurice Taylor, is the sixth to be appointed to administer the diocese of Galloway since the restoration of the hierarchy in 1878. His antecedents in occupying this historic bishopric go back therefore to St Ninian, the first bishop of Galloway, the see of Candida Casa, in AD *c.* 397.

Church Heritage Sites in
the Rhins of Galloway

The Rhins area is the most south-westerly part of Galloway and Scotland. It lies some 23 kilometres, or 14 miles, westwards across Luce Bay from the Machars peninsula, where Whithorn is located, and where St Ninian, the first bishop in Scotland, built the first stone church about the year AD 397. The proximity of the Rhins to Whithorn would lead to it being reached early in the missionary work of St Ninian and his co-workers, at the end of the 4th century or the beginning of the 5th century.

Evidence to support this early extension of Christianity to the Rhins is provided by the ancient, Christian, sculptured stones, preserved at Kirkmadrine. Apart from one older one at Whithorn, Kirkmadrine has the oldest existing Christian stone in the whole of Scotland. This stone has been dated to the 5th century. It is the commemorative burial stone for three priests, and is delicately inscribed in Latin.

From the 5th century, therefore, the Catholic Church has been an integral part of the life of the Rhins community in Galloway. For some eleven and a half centuries, up to the Reformation in 1560, churches and chapels and other religious institutions were built in different parts of the Rhins, to provide the Mass and the sacraments, and cater for the spiritual needs and welfare of the people.

By the time of the Reformation there were two abbeys, eight other parish churches, and as many as another thirty-four chapels. The existence of so many chapels may be attributed to a number of factors: they would be erected at sites of burial-grounds, or to serve the needs of communities at a distance from the parish church, or have been provided as a benefice by a local patron, or built simply as an expression of faith and devotion by the local populace. Although documents and records, mainly dating from the medieval period, are available for the abbeys and parish churches, they are rarely available for the many lesser chapels, but tradition, surviving place names and sometimes extant remains, combine generally to provide sufficient authentication for all but seven of them.

The remains of some of these centres of worship survive to this day — a precious reminder of the richness of the Christian heritage of the Rhins. These remains from the past combine with our own contemporary witness to the long, enduring, tradition of Christianity in this area.

As in the whole of life experience, the Church life and religious life of the people has had its peaks and troughs. But the ever-newness of Christ infuses his Church, and in its history we see a holy, sustaining metabolism at work. The Church's continued history through the centuries is in itself a sacrament, a sign, of Christ's presence and association with his people.

The past should not be forgotten. It is a part of us. It is part of our identity.

In the Rhins, then, the Church has a very prominent place in that which constitutes our heritage. We share a Christian heritage. It is for this reason that it is worth recording the places, the remains, the story, and the inherent richness of that heritage.

Historical precision is possible in some cases, but, in others, time and the ravages of history have blurred such exactitude, sometimes obscuring it. But there is much evidence and sufficient detail to see the tapestry of Church development, and appreciate the Christian life and commitment of the people of the Rhins through the centuries.

South Rhins

Kirkmadrine Parish Church

Kirkmaiden Parish Church

St Buite's Monastery (?), Dunman

St Medana's Cave and Chapel

St Medran's Chapel, Cardryne

St Mary's Chapel, Maryport

St Laisren's Chapel, Kirkleish, Inshanks

Kildonan Chapel, Near Drummore

St Eochod's Chapel, Hallyholm/Kilstay

St Bride's Chapel, Kirkbride

St Ninian's Chapel, Chipperdingan

St Finian's Chapel, Killingeane

Kirkholm Chapel

Chapel Rossan

Killaser

Kirkmabreck

Kirkmagill

Kirklauchline

Kirkmadrine Parish Church

This is the oldest Christian site in the area of the Rhins. Its location is fairly central to the area, and from the gently rising vantage point one can look across Luce Bay and view the long Machars peninsula. It is a site within relatively easy reach of Whithorn. A church would most probably have been established here just after St Ninian and his followers had set up their first church at Whithorn in AD *c.* 397. So Kirkmadrine as a church centre probably dates from the 5th century. Indeed two of the ancient inscribed Christian stones found in the area have been dated as 5th century, providing some evidence for the early foundation of the church.

The collection of early Christian stone memorials and monuments preserved at Kirkmadrine suggests the early presence of a large monastery or missionary centre, which would have been contemporaneous with St Ninian's church at Whithorn. (T, 12-13)

The title of the church as Kirkmadrine has two interpretations. One is that it was dedicated to St Martin, the other that it was dedicated to St Mathurin.

Supportive of it being St Martin is the fact that the first church in the diocese of Galloway, at Whithorn, was dedicated to St Martin. St Martin of Tours would be known to St Ninian, the first bishop of Galloway. St Martin died in the year 397, was widely known and venerated, and many churches were named after him. Traditionally, too, each November in Scotland there is the Quarter Day of Martinmas. The name Martin is translated in Gaelic into *Matrainn*, and the oblique form is Matrin; this would evolve to Kirkmadrine, the church of Martin, by which it has come to be known and titled in Galloway.

MacQueen (Q2, 21) interprets Kirkmadrine as 'Church of my Draighne', but does not elaborate on this.

The claim that the church was named after St Mathurin of Sens is based on the fact that this saint was a Gaulish contemporary of St Martin of Tours, although less widely known and honoured.

The weight of opinion supports St Martin of Tours as being the patron saint of the church at Kirkmadrine.

The Christianising of the Rhins in those early times would have been centred at Kirkmadrine.

Through the ensuing centuries, other churches and chapels were erected in the Rhins area. By the 13th century, Kirkmadrine was a simple parish church, serving only a small district. And so it continued up to and just beyond the Reformation in the 16th century.

At this time it was referred to as the parish of Kirkmadrine or Toskerton, the latter seemingly being the name of a nearby hamlet. (The title 'Toskerton' seems to come from the Gaelic *tuaise-art-an*, meaning 'the northerly place'.)

According to the Testament of Prior Malcolm Fleming (Edinburgh Testaments, 30 March and 2 July 1569), Toskertoun or Kirkmadrine belonged to the Premonstratensian Priory of Whithorn at the period of the Reformation. Some further evidence of this is given by a deed, testifying that Canon Frederick Bruce was both Subprior of Whithorn and Vicar of Soulseat and Toskerton on 27 March 1558 (0, 53). It would seem that his tenure did not extend much beyond that date, because Thomas Acoltrane, a diocesan priest, is recorded as being Vicar of Kirkmadrine in 1558 (ibid 52). His appointment, in turn, lasted for only about one year. He was succeeded in March 1559 or 1560 by Michael Hawthorn, a priest of the Diocese of Galloway since 1549. So he was the incumbent Vicar of Kirkmadrine (Toskerton) just prior to and at the time of the Reformation, in 1560 (ibid 55).

John Dunbar, possibly tacksman, was reader in 1569, 1571-2, 1574 (z, 149). Michael Hawthorn is recorded as vicar and reader at Toskerton in 1572-4 (o, 55). Nicol (or Michael) Dungalson (minister of Longcastle) had the oversight of this church in 1574 (z, 149). Michael Hawthorn is recorded as minister at Toskerton in 1576, and as late vicar of the place in 1585. He was also evidently in charge of the parish church at Borgue, near Kirkcudbright. (o, 55)

An important personage at Kirkmadrine at this important transitional time in the country was Michael Hawthorn. He had served as a Catholic priest of the Diocese of Galloway for at least eleven years before the Reformation, at which time he was vicar of Kirkmadrine parish. He was notary at Wigtown in 1561-2 (ibid 55). Hew Scott says that

> Michael Hawthorn, who had been in orders in the Popish Church, and held the vicarage of Borgue, entered Reader at Tosquartoun [Kirkmadrine of Toskerton] at Lammas [August] 1572. (x, 773)

It may be that he deferred committing himself to the reformed church in this way until it was clear that it had prevailed. He may, equally, have been prompted by fear of deprivation, since it was proposed in 1572, and passed into law in the following year, that clergy who would not accept the reformed Confession of Faith should be deprived of their benefice (o, 43-44). He is recorded as vicar and reader at Toskerton in the period 1572-4 and minister in 1576 (ibid 55). In 1576 he had charge and responsibility for the combination of Kirkmadrine of Toskerton, Kirkmaiden (in the Rhins), Leswalt, Kirkcolm and Clayshant. Retaining these multiple charges, he moved in 1580 or 1585 to Killemorie or Kirkcolm (x, 759 & 773) and it would seem it was at this latter place that he died in 1585. (ibid 759)

Kirkmadrine church continued to be used therefore by the constituted Church that emerged in Scotland at the time of the Reformation in 1560.

Some 3 miles (5 kilometres) further north, the medieval church of St Stephen, at Stoneykirk, became the centre of parish life, and eventually, on or before 1618, the parish of St Stephen's, Stoneykirk, subsumed the old parishes of Kirkmadrine and Clayshant. Scott (x, 773) states that Kirkmadrine was united to Stoneykirk parish before 20 June 1618.

Timothy Pont (*c.* 1560-1630) surveyed virtually the whole of Scotland between 1584 and 1601. He was surveying in Galloway *c.* 1595.

Robert Gordon of Straloch, as cartographic editor, used Pont's manuscript maps to produce the maps in *Atlas Novus* by Johan Blaeu in Amsterdam in 1654. In this edition, the map showing the Rhins area of Galloway contains a number of symbolic drawings of churches with their appended names. The suggestion is that these are intact, not ruined, church buildings in 1595. Kirkmadrine is included and is named as 'K. Makdrym'.

Similarly, the 1687 original map of Scotland by Robert Morden, reproduced in 1695, shows K. Macdrym at the location of Kirkmadrine.

In General William Roy's 'Mull of Galloway' maps, *c.* 1747, Kirk MaDryn is shown at the site presently known as Kirkmadrine.

All of these three maps suggest an intact church building at Kirkmadrine up to *c.* 1747.

In 1781 John Ainslie surveyed the County of Wigtownshire. He published a map of the area, dated 2 May 1782. In the Rhins area he locates and prints the 'Ruins of Kirkmadrine'.

From this evidence it would seem that the church of Kirkmadrine ceased to be used and became ruinous between *c.* 1747 and 1781. McKerlie (H, II, 162) writes in 1877:

> Only a portion of the eastern gable and the side walls now remain. It is to be regretted that the rubbish in the interior is not cleared out and other measures taken for its preservation

Thus a church stood at Kirkmadrine, serving the local community, from the 5th century until the 18th century — a remarkable span of thirteen centuries.

The churchyard had continued as a burial ground over this long period. A stone wall nearly encloses the churchyard today.

The property is now part of the Ardwell Estate. At the end of the 19th century, Lady McTaggart of Ardwell initiated restoration work. She arranged for the building of a private family-vault chapel at Kirkmadrine. This incorporated some earlier masonry, most notably at the east end, and may have preserved the ground plan of the former church. (The aisle measures 12.7 metres by 5.6 metres within walls 0.9 metre thick), (c, 28). This restored church was modelled also on the 12th-century Romanesque church at Cruggleton, near Whithorn, in the Machars. Several family members are buried within this family-vault chapel. This chapel stands today at Kirkmadrine as a memorial to a long and proud heritage.

The Kirkmadrine Stones

At the west end of the private chapel at Kirkmadrine there is a large recess, fronted by a protective glass window. Within this recess are preserved eight, old, Christian, sculptured stones, kept under the care of the Secretary of State for Scotland under the agency of Historic Scotland. This arrangement ensures that these stones are always accessible for viewing by the public.

Two of these stones are dated to the 5th century, another of late 6th-century date, and the remainder range in date from the 8th to the 12th century. These stones are of very important historical significance. Indeed, with the exception of one older Christian stone at Whithorn, which is dated *c.* 450, the two 5th-century stones at Kirkmadrine are believed to be the oldest inscribed Christian stone monuments in Scotland. These two oldest stones at Kirkmadrine had, over the centuries, come to be used as gateposts at the churchyard entrance (E, 154). When, in the 19th century, their significance was realised, they were moved to their present protective location. They bear the marks of the holes which were used to support the gates.

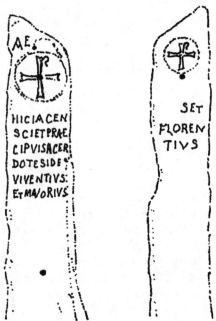

The two oldest Kirkmadrine Stones — 5th century

Both of these oldest Kirkmadrine stones are of indurated schist.

The principal one stands 2.06 metres tall, and is some 0.41 metres wide and 0.10 metre in thickness. On the front face of this stone, inscribed in Latin, are the words:

HIC IACEN

SCI ET PRAE

CIPUIS SACER

DOTES IDE

VIVENTIUS

ET MAVORIUS

Either through the use of abbreviations or defacement through weathering or abuse, this inscription should read:

HIC IACEN[T] S[AN]C[T]I ET PRAECIPUI SACERDOTES IDE[S] VIVENTIUS ET MAVORIUS

This is translated as:

HERE LIE THE HOLY AND CHIEF [OR EXCELLENT] PRIESTS IDES VIVENTIUS AND MAVORIUS

The incompleteness or otherwise of the word or words formed by the letters IDE[S], terminating the fourth line, may be translated as either — Here lie holy and excellent priests Ides [or *id est* = that is to say], Viventius and Mavorius (or Maiorius). (E, 156)

Between the top of the stone and its Latin inscription there is an engraved Chi-Rho monogram. The letters Chi(χ) and Rho(ρ), the first two letters in Greek of Christ's name, are commonly used as an abbreviation. The Chi letter is sometimes eighth-turned to make a vertical-horizontal cross, and the letter Rho superimposed on the vertical with its loop extension at the top right, (shown on the illustration of the stone). The Chi-Rho monogram on this stone is enclosed within an engraved circle. Above the circle are two inscribed letters, A E, part of an original four-letter inscription, which would read A ET Ω, Alpha and Omega, the first and last letters of the Greek alphabet, signifying the Beginning and the End, a description of God.

The second, later 5th-century, companion stone measures 2.13 metres in height, 0.36 metre in width, and 0.08 metre in thickness. On its face at the top it, too, has an inscribed Chi-Rho monogram within a circle. Below this there are three lines of capital letters in Latin, which read:

S ET

FLOREN

TIUS

The original letters before the first S are no longer discernible on the stone. Translated, the inscription reads:

...S AND FLORENTIUS

The letters here are more rudely carved than on the first stone, and the inscription consisting as it does of the two names coupled by the conjunction 'and', without anything preceding, suggests that it has been intended to be read continuously with the inscription on the first stone (E, 156).

The Kirkmadrine Heritage

The preserved stones at Kirkmadrine reveal much. They tell us that at that early period, as early as the 5th century, the Church was already established in the Rhins area of Galloway. Such development would be expected after the establishment of the first church at Whithorn in AD *c.* 397. The 5th-century dating of two of these memorial stones indicates a Christian burial ground at Kirkmadrine, with a church and a community now with the expertise capable of preparing and inscribing such memorial stones. It may be argued that in the absence of such an established centre in the Rhins, such esteemed Church personnel would have been transferred back to their central residence at Whithorn for burial.

Not only do the stones provide evidence of the early establishment and growth of the Church in the Rhins area, they also provide evidence of the religious disposition and nature of the Church that was being established. The inscription on the oldest stone memorial at Kirkmadrine refers to three 'sacerdotes', that is, three priests. Thus, the Catholic Faith, with its central act of worship, the Holy Sacrifice of the Mass, was being made available to the local populace through the ministry of these and other priests.

With knowledge of Christ, his teaching, his life, death and resurrection, with knowledge of the Church which he established upon Peter, with entry into the life of Christ and his Church through baptism, there would be a sharing in the corporate and central act of worship, a sharing that Christ commissioned, when, at the Last Supper, he instituted the Eucharist and instructed, 'Do this as a memorial of me.' (Luke 22:19)

Baptism and the other sacraments would be extended to those open and disposed to receive them. This would be an integral part of the normal work of the priests. In this way they would found other churches, like the one at Kirkmadrine, extending the area of influence of the Church, building up parish and community Christian life, sustaining the people's Faith by providing for their participation in the Eucharistic Sacrifice of the Mass, by sacramental administration, and by their evangelisation, teaching and general charitable work.

So, the Faith was planted in the Rhins, at Kirkmadrine. It rooted and grew. It developed from there. But it continued at Kirkmadrine from the 5th to the 16th century — some eleven centuries of Catholic life and tradition. It continued in a different Christian form after the 1560 Reformation in Scotland.

Postscript

An interesting postscript to this story concerns the last Catholic priest, Michael Hawthorne, resident at Kirkmadrine at the time of the Reformation, in 1560. As described earlier, he continued his ministry within the jurisdiction of the new Reformed Church of Scotland, and died in 1585 still in Church service. Catholicism, ceasing to be a proscribed religion in the 19th century, was re-established at Stranraer, with the institution of St Joseph's Parish in 1846. Parishioners from this parish, with two priests and visitors from other parishes, together with some other non-Catholic fellow Christians, gathered at Kirkmadrine on Sunday, 6 September 1992. With the kind permission of Mrs Faith Brewis, of Ardwell Estate, the 19th-century family-vault chapel was used to accommodate the assembly on a wet afternoon. Mass was celebrated, honouring the heritage of holiness associated with Kirkmadrine over a span of some fifteen centuries. This would be the first Mass to be celebrated there since the time of the Reformation, before which time Mass had been celebrated there for more than a thousand years. It healed a wound. It united the past with the present. The Mass sealed us together in Christ. It was a joy for all who were present. Amongst those attending this Mass at Kirkmadrine was a lady from Kirkcudbright, Mrs Agatha Ann Taylor, whose maiden name is Hawthorn. Family records show her to be distantly related to Father Michael Hawthorne. So not only was there a profound sense of religious continuity with the past as Mass was celebrated, but there was also present some semblance even of human family continuity, which only added to the memorable nature of the celebration.

Access to Kirkmadrine: *OS Map Ref NX 0801 4839*

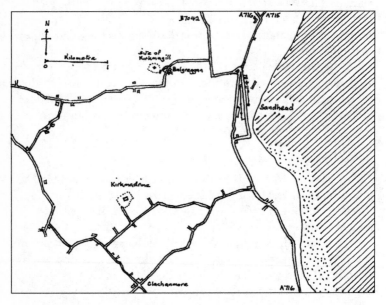

There is all-year access to the site at Kirkmadrine. It is well sign-posted from the A716 road, about a kilometre south of Sandhead. The historic stones are always on view in their glass-protected niche. There is no access to the 19th-century private family-vault chapel, except with permission from the Ardwell Estate. There is presently some limited parking space for cars.

Kirkmaiden Parish Church

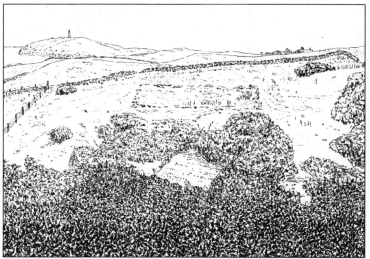

This parish church was named after St Medana. Locally, through time, her name became Medan and the church came to be titled Kirkmaiden. MacQueen (Q2, 21) interprets Kirkmaiden as 'church of my Etain', but does not elaborate on this. St Medana's period of residence in the cave on the nearby south Rhins coast was during the 8th century. The small chapel extension at the cave took place sometime in the Middle Ages. It was probably some time between the 8th and 12th centuries when this nearby parish church of Kirkmaiden was built.

Todd (F, 54), in his account of this parish, says that among the sprinkling of old churches in this neighbourhood, Kirkbride and the old Kirk at the Mull, called we suppose St Medan's Kirk, appear to have been the most modern.

The remains of the old Kirkmaiden Church are situated in a little glen with a stream, called the Kirk Burn, which spills into Luce Bay at a little inlet known as Portankill (which means 'the harbour of the chapel'). The church site is little more than 0.5 kilometre north of the Mull of Galloway Farm, and about 1.0 kilometre north-east of St Medana's cave-chapel.

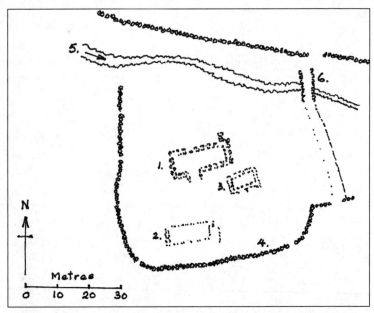

Kirkmaiden: (1) Remains of Kirkmaiden Medieval Parish Church; (2) Structural remains, possibly a building; (3) Undetermined structural remains; (4) Stone wall, enclosing burial ground; (5) Kirk Burn; (6) Stone Bridge.

Nothing remains of the upper walls of the church; but some parts of the lower walls or foundations peep through grassy mound lines, which clearly show its location, shape and size. Like other early churches, it lies on a west to east axis, is rectangular in shape, and measures about 15.5 metres by 6.0 metres internally. There is a broken dry-stone wall defining the boundary of the churchyard burial ground. Apart from the church, within the burial ground there are signs of three other rectangular structures, of unknown date and purpose, the largest of which, on the south side, measuring 15 metres in overall length, may be a building.

McKerlie (H, II, 39) says, 'Close to the site of the old church is St Catherine's Croft. It stands on Mull farm.' This St Catherine's Croft may be one of the outbuildings which formerly stood within the old churchyard. Alternatively, it may have been sited actually at the present Mull of Galloway Farm, which is about 0.5 kilometre south of the site of the old Kirkmaiden Church. It may be that the croft building itself has become integrated within the complex of buildings making up the farm. An aerial photograph shows the remains of an old footpath from the south-east corner of Kirkmaiden Churchyard going southwards to the east side of Mull of Galloway Farm. It is interesting to note that there is an old well in the vicinity known as Tibbertiekite. This name is from the Gaelic, *Tiobar tighe cait*, meaning 'The Well of Kate's House'. This well is situated about 0.7 kilometre south-west of Mull of Galloway Farm and about 0.4 kilometre south-east of West Cairngaan Farm.

It is probable that this St Mary's Croft was a residence erected by the Premonstratensian Canons from Soulseat Abbey, when they officially took charge of Kirkmaiden Parish Church in 1393.

At that time Christendom was acclaiming St Catherine of Siena (1347-80), one of the illustrious saints of the medieval period. She grew up in Siena, and received the habit of the third order of St Dominic. She worked among the poor of Siena. She was renowned for her temporal and spiritual works of charity. The unity and welfare of the Church was of great concern to her. She was instrumental in persuading Pope Gregory XI to leave Avignon and return to Rome. Her writing was extensive. She was canonised a saint in 1461, and declared Doctor of the Church in 1970.

McKerlie (ibid 138) says, 'The ancient Parish Church was dedicated to St Catherine' [mentioning that there was another chapel to the same saint in Stoneykirk parish]. This may have been a dedication made also at the time of the appropriation of the parish church by the Premonstratensian Canons of Soulseat Abbey *c.* 1393. As with St Catherine's Croft, the Kirkmaiden Parish Church could then have been dedicated to the 14th-century saint, St Catherine of Siena.

Scott (Y, II, 340) states that St Katherine's Chapel was at St Katherine's Croft, but does not say which saint of that name.

McKerlie (s, 7) says that this church at Kirkmaiden, 'from its antiquity, must have been dedicated to St Catherine of Alexandria':

According to a legend, she was a maiden martyred at Alexandria under Maxentius, but there is no evidence for this before the 9th century. Her alleged relics have been enshrined for the last thousand years in the Orthodox monastery of Mt Sinai. In art she is represented with the spiked wheel of her martyrdom, or arguing with the pagan philosophers. Nothing definite seems to be known about her life (I, 116).

Since about the 10th century or earlier she was venerated in the East, but from the time of the Crusades until the 18th century her popularity was even greater in the west. Numerous churches were dedicated in her honour (J, IV, 420).

It may then be the case that when Kirkmaiden Parish Church was built, a considerable time before it was taken over by Soulseat Abbey, it may have been dedicated to St Catherine of Alexandria.

Kirkmaiden was the parish church for this southernmost part of the Rhins.

The earliest written record referring to Kirkmaiden dates from 1386, when Walter, an apostolic delegate, annexed the church to Soulseat. A charter by Pope Clement VII on 15 July 1393, approved of Finlay, abbot of Soulseat Abbey, securing annexation of the parish church of Kirkmaiden in 'le Rynnis'. (K, 92)

Reid (ibid 92) writes:

> The moment was appropriate because Finlay Ahannay had just resigned the living. Ahannay cannot have held Kirkmaiden long if he was the same person as the Finlay Ahannay 'of Scotland', a canon of Whithorn and for three years a scholar of civil law, who in 1390 petitioned for a benefice in the gift of the bishop and convent of Whithorn.

From that time, *c.* 1393, up until the period of the Reformation in 1560, Kirkmaiden parish continued to be served by priests, all of whom were Canons of the Premonstratensian Order from Soulseat Abbey. Canon Cornelius Macmaken was one such vicar at Kirkmaiden in the 14th century. After an interval he was succeeded by Canon Gilbert Makdonyl. (ibid 92)

Writing about this medieval period, MacQueen (Q2, 31) notes that the Edgars' barony, centred on Drummore, may have extended to the farm of Creechan, near Maryport. Later, the Gordons succeeded to the barony, their boundary including more southerly parts of the Mull of Galloway. He remarks, 'The Edgars' church was probably Kildonan, and the Gordons' Kirkmaiden. Kirkleish was probably the church for the barony of Barncorkrie.' He also mentions, just further north, the long-established family of McDouall of Logan, with a nearby church at Killingeane. He adds,

> All four baronies were included in the parish of Kirkmaiden, so Kildonan, Kirkleish and probably Kirkbride (near which is a field Kirkbride Kirkyaird with remains of buildings) and Killingeane may have functioned as chapels-of-ease, providing for the needs of a parish which, as one Vicar of Kirkmaiden in the middle 15th century ruefully observed, was [quoting Reid 1960:93] 'eight Italian miles around and very populous'.

After the Reformation it is recorded that John White, possibly a canon of Soulseat, was vicar on 14 May 1562 and in 1567-72, was reader in 1574, and was deceased vicar pensioner before 3 March 1580. John Gibson (minister of Clayshant) had the oversight of Kirkmaiden Church in 1574 (z, 149-50).

At the time of the Reformation the parish church was taken over and then used for Reformed Church services up until at least 1639, when a new church, still existing, was erected at a new Kirkmaiden site, one kilometre north-west of Drummore. This replacement church, McKerlie (H, II, 139) says, though commenced in 1638, was not completed until probably 1650, because of a 'dispute amongst the heritors'.

Pont's survey of *c.* 1595, from which the John Blaeu maps of 1654 were published, indicates a church, which he names Kirkmadin, in the area of the present ancient ruins.

After its abandonment in the 17th century the ancient Kirkmaiden Church became ruinous. In 1687, Robert Morden shows it on his map as C. Madyn, but does not indicate its state. It is not mentioned in General William Roy's map of *c.* 1747, nor in Ainslie's map based on his 1782 survey, and again it is not mentioned in Johnson's map of 1826. But 19th- and 20th-century Ordnance Survey maps indicate this old Kirkmaiden Church site.

Two interesting reminiscences are recorded by Todd (F, 55). Writing about St Medan's Kirk [Kirkmaiden] at the Mull of Galloway, he says,

> though the building is all gone, the foundation and the old churchyard is still enclosed and undisturbed. About 70 years ago (*c.* 1784) an attempt was made to bring it under the plough. The horses were yoked into the plough, and all in readiness to commence, when the horses took fright and ran off, breaking plough and harness. No attempt has been since made upon its sacred solitude.
>
> The churchyard, though enclosed, has not been of late used, except in the rare instance of interring a seaman's mangled corpse, cast ashore near the place.

As described in the section dealing with Kildonan (South Rhins), a cross-incised stone slab of Early Christian date, now in the National Museum of Antiquities of Scotland, is said to have come either from this church, or from Kildonan chapel, near Drummore.

Access: *OS Map Ref NX 1385 3243*

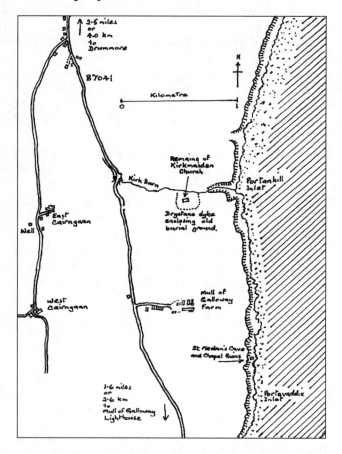

At present the Kirkmaiden Church site is not signposed. From the field gate just south of the Kirk Burn bridge on the B7041, about 600 metres north of the Mull of Galloway Farm, proceed eastwards on foot across the field for about 400 metres, keeping to the fringe of the field above the little glen. The foundational remains of Kirkmaiden Church are within a sloping, roughly rectangular area, bounded by a dry-stone wall

St Buite's Monastery (?), Dunman

Not necessarily because of authenticity but because a single source states the possibility, reference is made to a monastic settlement at Dunman. McKerlie (s, 9-11) speaks of an old holy well at Muntloch, on Kilbuie moss, and says that the name Kilbuie offers the suggestion that a 'cell' dedicated to St Buite the Monk may have had a site here.

St Buite (or Buithe or Boethius), who died in the year 521 (1, 104), was a Scot, whom McKerlie claims was Irish. Having spent some years in Italy and elsewhere on the Continent, he returned to Scotland, founded a monastery, and evangelised the Picts. There is a tradition that he restored the health of a Pictish king by his prayers, and was rewarded with the gift of the royal fort where this took place. He founded a monastery there. Dunnichen, in Angus, is thought to be the site of St Buite's foundation. Near it are still to be seen the remains of an ancient fortress known as Carbuddo (*Castrum Butthi*), or Caer Buido (Buite's Fort), or Kirkbuddo.

McKerlie (s, 10-11) writes:

Here in the Mull of Galloway was a territory of the Picts (the Irish Picts or Cruithne), and on the western side remains of their strongholds; whether or no the scene of St Buite's miracle and labours, they are very suggestive. There is Fort Duniehinnie on the Mull of Logan, joined to the mainland by a neck of rock, and lashed by the waves of the Irish Sea; a little further south, an important one on Crummag Head. It is, however, on the rocky height of Dunman, of over 500 feet (152 metres), which rises sheer from the sea, that are found the remains of a great fortress.

It might well be the site of St Buite's Monastery, whence his own country would be often in view. Behind the outer wall or enceinte on the landward side, with its cyclopean blocks of stone, extends Kilbuie Moss. Dunman is said to mean Dun Monadh, Fort of the Hill in Gaelic idiom, and may have replaced manach or monk, which also applies to Port Mona, the Monk's Port — a traditional name.

Todd (F, 42), writing in 1854, says:

[Dunman is] a high hill in the south-western corner of the parish, remarkable for the remains of an old fortification on its top. Fortified hills were called Duns, and the name Dunman seems to be derived from the Gaelic Dun-monadh, signifying the mountain fort, or a fort on a moss-covered mountain. The fortifications on its top are said to be the remains of a Pictish encampment.

Whilst not totally discounting McKerlie's suggestion, it seems that tradition favours St Buite being connected with Kirkbuddo, in Angus, on the eastern side of Scotland, rather than Dunman, in the south-western Rhins.

Access: *OS Map Ref NX 0975 3345*

Remote, cross-country site. Area can be approached by car from Drummore via Damnaglaur. Final kilometre or so on foot.

St Medana's Cave and Chapel

St Medana is of the 8th century. She was of Irish birth. As a maiden, she left Ireland and settled in Galloway, where she spent time living in a cave in the South Rhins, overlooking Luce Bay and near the Mull of Galloway. In the present-day Rhins this saint is referred to as St Medan.

There is a lesser suggestion that the saint connected with this place is not Medana but Modwenna, who is sometimes called Medana, or Edana, Monyna, Merryn, and, in French, Modivene. Four or five saints of this name are listed in different menologies, but their lives are hopelessly confused. Two seem to have been more important than the rest: St Modwenna, who succeeded St Hilda as abbess of Whitby (died *c.* 695); St Modwenna, abbess of Polesworth in Warwickshire (died *c.* 900). It is very much more probable that the saint associated with this cave in the Rhins is not Modwenna but Medana. The saint also has association with the neighbouring Machars peninsula, across Luce Bay. In that area, near Monreith, there is a St Medana's Well and a nearby church ruin with Norman period features, but perhaps older than that, and called Kirkmaiden.

From the time of St Medana the cave here in the South Rhins has been a place of devotion for pilgrims and interested visitors.

The cave itself is a triangular recess in the rock face, measuring 3.4 metres in length and up to 2.8 metres in width. A clay-bonded stone wall, 7.3 metres high and 1.0 metre thick, is built across the mouth of the cave, and this incorporates a doorway giving access to the interior. The doorway is now supported by stanchions and beams of railway bars.

Sometime in the early Middle Ages a stone-built chapel was extended outwards from the cave. It is trapezium-shaped, being somewhat wider at the front end than at the cave end at the back. It is 4.7 metres in length. Viewing it from outside, the left side of the chapel consists of the rock face jutting out from the cave. On the right side it is again mostly rock face jutting out from the cave, but with some supplementary stone-walling on top. Part of the north-eastern entrance wall is still standing. These chapel walls are of lime-mortared stone. The front wall has incorporated an internally-splayed window and an entrance doorway, which is now an opening 1.3 metres wide. Another small section of retaining wall has stood to the left of the doorway entrance to the chapel.

This chapel may have had a loft and probably a lean-to, slated roof. Nothing now remains of the roofing.

Over the centuries, from 1560 until 1870, the chapel ceased to be maintained. Besides becoming a ruin, it has also been pillaged by treasure seekers, who at times have dug into the floor of the chapel and cave.

Coins, metalwork, animal and human bones, and the statuette of a draped, female figure were found during official excavations carried out in the year 1870. At that time it was reported that, when some of the soil within the inner chapel area had been removed, a large stone was discovered measuring 1.2 metres long, 0.6 metres high and 0.6 metres broad, which was built up so as to form a sort of platform under the splayed front window. This description and the position of the stone indicates an altar for the celebration of Mass.

Before further examination of the contents revealed by this official excavation could be completed, a Sunday intervened, and it is reported that on that day an ill-disposed mob interfered with the cave and its contents. They threw down portions of the wall, smashed up the draped figure as a relic of popery, and cast it with the discovered bones and most of the slates into the sea. They carried off the brass ornaments, nails, buttons and coins that had been unearthed (E, 51).

In *c.* 1595 Timothy Pont carried out his surveying of the Galloway area. Robert Gordon used Pont's manuscripts to produce maps published by Johan Blaeu in 1654. Maidin's Coave (Maiden's Cave) appears in the map of the Rhins area. Medana, become Medan, is interpreted as Maiden in this map. So by *c.* 1595 we have the use of Maiden for Medana. By this time another nearby parish church had been built, called Kirkmadin (Kirkmaiden), which is described in a preceding section.

Some 27 metres south-east along the rocky coastline from St Medana's cave and chapel there are three associated holy wells. These are three natural cavities filled by the sea at high water of ordinary tides. A local custom is reported of people specially visiting chapel, cave and wells on the first Sunday of May, a day referred to as Co or Cove Sunday.

Access: *OS Map Ref NX 1436 3165*

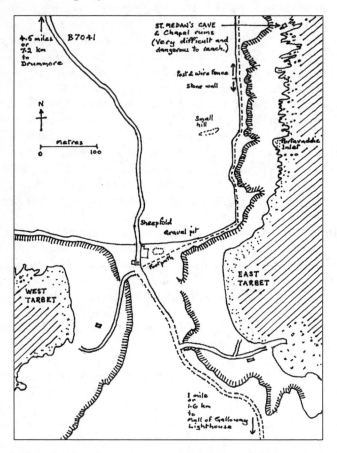

At present the cave is not signposted. It can be reached on foot, with some difficulty, from East Tarbet, near the Mull of Galloway. There is a rough footpath northwards along the top of the cliffs or steep slopes of the rocky coastline of Luce Bay. The cave below is not visible from above. There are one or two places where a somewhat difficult descent can be made. Perhaps in time to come, access may be made easier.

St Medran's Chapel, Cardryne

This chapel is said to have stood in the vicinity of Cardryne Farm, some 4.5 kilometres north-west of the Mull of Galloway (c, 26). There are no visible remains. Todd (F, 54) says that Kirkdrain, or Kirkdryne, was one of the six main old kirks in this southern area of the Rhins.

In the new Statistical Account of Scotland in 1841 (L, 199), Kirkdryne or Kirkdrain is listed as a pre-Reformation place of worship.

Scott (Y, 11, 340) says there was a St Medran's Chapel at Kirk Dryne.

McKerlie (H, 11, 139), writing about the old Kirkmaiden church near the Mull of Galloway Farm, states: 'The manse and glebe were on the farm of Cardrain, about a mile from the church.'

Although the parish was supplied by John Quheit [White] from 1574 to 1579 and Thomas Wricht in 1580, a report (L, 199-200), in 1841, referring to Kirkdryne or Kirkdrain states:

> Here was the residence of Mr John Callender, the first Protestant minister of the (Kirkmaiden) parish, though his place of worship was about a mile distant, on the farm of Mull, the old church already mentioned, and said by Chalmers to be dedicated to St Medan.

Todd (F, 178), writing in 1854, adds:

His Manse and glebe were on the Farm of Kirkdrain about a mile distant from the Kirk. The walls of the Manse formed part of the walls of the Farmer's dwelling house about 45 years ago.

This minister took up office in 1607. It would seem that this location for the manse would date from about 1607 until *c.* 1650, when the new replacement Kirkmaiden Church came into use in its new location one kilometre north-west of Drummore.

In this area of the South Rhins there are the two farm properties, Cardryne and Cardrain, within a kilometre of each other. The likeness of the names and the proximity of each to the other may have led to some confusion as to which is the location for the former old kirk, St Medran's Chapel. That being so, it may be that if the 17th-century manse was located at Cardrain, then it may have incorporated the old St Medran's Chapel, which might have been at that site rather than, as supposed, at Cardryne.

St Medran was a disciple of St Kieran of Saghir in the 6th century. Since St Medran was Irish, it would seem that the chapel dedicated to him would be of Celtic origin, perhaps between the 7th and the 11th centuries.

Access: Cardryne *OS Map Ref NX c117 324*
Cardrain *OS Map Ref NX 1245 3190*

Cardryne is reached by a secondary road, going west then south from Damnaglaur, which is near Drummore.

Cardrain is reached by taking the Mull of Galloway B7041 road south from Damnaglaur. After two kilometres, take the secondary road south-westwards, via Cairngaan, to Cardrain.

St Mary's Chapel, Maryport

Timothy Pont's survey of Galloway in *c.* 1595 resulted in the production of maps by John Blaeu in 1654. The map of the Rhins area indicates a sizeable religious building at Maryport, between Drummore and the Mull of Galloway. This building was a chapel. It is stated in the Imperial Gazetteer of Scotland in 1854 (R, 262) and by McKerlie in 1877 (H, II, 140) and by Scott in 1950 (Y, VIII, 189) that the chapel was dedicated to the Virgin Mary. This is in keeping with the retained name of Maryport for this quiet little bay. The chapel was never a parish church — the parish church being Kirkmaiden, two kilometres south of Maryport.

There is a suggestion that this chapel belonged to a religious community, perhaps a convent of nuns. McKerlie (S, 8) states that such a religious community was established there in 1190. Cowan and Easson (B), in 1976, do not include or refer to a religious community at Maryport in their authoritative book, *The Medieval Religious Houses — Scotland*. In the records that are available for nuns' foundations in the Galloway area during the 12th, 13th and 14th centuries, there is only one community of nuns listed; that was the community of Benedictine Nuns, founded *c.* 1174 at Lincluden Priory, Dumfries. In a papal letter of 7 May 1389, this nunnery is designated as 'of the Cluniac Order' (B, 143). It would seem that if any nuns were resident at Maryport, they may have withdrawn from there before the period of the Reformation; at the latest they are not likely to have continued for long after 1560.

Whether or not it was a convent chapel, Symson (G, 65) reports the chapel at Maryport as in ruins in 1684. Ainslie's map of 1782, based on his 1781 survey of the area, indicates a building at Maryport, but does not depict it as a religious building. Today, no vestiges of the chapel nor convent survive.

Cailiness Point is a headland 1.5 kilometres north-west of Maryport. McKerlie (H, II, 153) says of this promontory,

> Pont renders Kilness or Killiness as Kellyness, which there is little doubt is a corruption of Kil from Cill, a church or cell, and Ness, from the Norse *nes*, a headland. The ancient chapel(s) of Saint Medan and Saint Mary were nearby, from one of which the name Chapel point was no doubt given.

Access: *OS Map Ref NX 141 344*

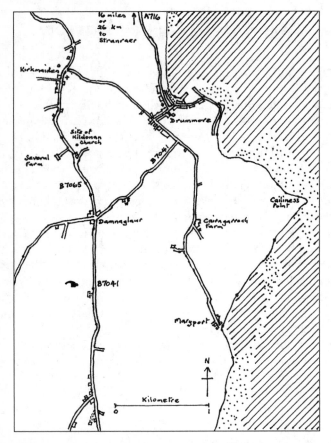

Maryport is accessible by road. It lies a little more than two kilometres south of Drummore. As stated earlier, there are no extant remains to be seen of the chapel nor of any medieval convent.

St Laisren's Chapel, Kirkleish, Inshanks

St Laisren's Chapel was situated here, in the foreground field.

There are no visible remains of this chapel, which is sometimes referred to as Kirkleish. It formerly stood to the west of Inshanks Fell, a hill about 1.25 kilometres west of Damnaglaur, and about 0.8 kilometre north of Inshanks Farm (c, 28).

In the New Statistical Account of Scotland in 1841 (L, 199), Kirkleish is listed as a pre-Reformation place of worship.

Todd (F, 54) refers to Kirk-cleish as one of the six main old kirks in this southern area of the Rhins.

McKerlie (H, II, 141) says:

In the Ordnance Map (1856 edn. 1 inch to the mile), there is also the site of a chapel called Kirkleish, and a well at Muntloch, some distance south. That a chapel with that name ever existed we do not credit. The churches and chapels were almost as a rule named after Saints, and no such Saint as Leish will be found in any calendar.

However, the chapel is said to have been dedicated to St Laisren, who is also known as Molaisse or Laserian. The history of St Laisren is very uncertain. He is said to have spent several years at Iona, then further time in a monastery at Leighlin, in Northumbria. On his second visit to Rome he was consecrated bishop and appointed papal legate for Ireland, where he settled the paschal controversy in favour of the Roman date for keeping Easter. He seems to have again returned to Leighlin, in Northumbria, where he died in the year 639. It could be the case that this saint would have passed through the Rhins area on his journeys to and from Ireland.

Scott (Y, II, 340) states that St Lashrean's chapel was at Kirkleish.

The Celtic chapel named after St Laisren at Inshanks Fell would most probably have been founded early in the period of the 7th to the 13th centuries.

MacQueen (Q2, 21, 31) provides an alternative intepretation of the title Kirkleish. He says this represents the Gaelic *kirk ghille Iosa*, 'church of Jesus' lad'. He adds that in the medieval period Kirkleish was probably the church for the barony of Barncorkrie and lay within the parish of Kirkmaiden. So Kirkleish would act as a chapel-of-ease, and be served by a priest from Kirkmaiden parish church.

Commenting on the name Inshanks, McKerlie (H, II, 154-5) states:

> Inshanks is spelled Inschaes by Pont. This may be from the Gaelic *Innse*, an inch or plain, and the Cymric *Sinach*, a landmark, a ridge, or perhaps from the Gaelic *Innseach*, for peninsula.

He adds that the word Inch was used here as in other parts of Scotland to places inland.

On the western side of Inshanks Fell the land slopes down to a wide basin type of plain. Water is presently taken away through large iron drainpipes, probably dating back a century. In the hollow of the field, in which St Laisren's Chapel is said to have stood, the presence of marsh grass and boggy ground suggests that, before drainage was installed, water would have collected in this hollow to form a little loch. This would account for the chapel being sited on slightly higher ground on the north side of this hollow. The chapel may actually then have been situated at the northern side of that little loch. The latter is perhaps indicated by an indefinite detail at the location in Roy's *c.* 1747 map.

Presently there are no dwellings near the chapel site, but Roy's map, *c.* 1747, and Ainslie's map, 1782, indicate a number of dwellings in the area. MacQueen (Q2, 21) reports in 1973, 'The last remains of a small stone building are still visible'. Sadly, these too have gone now; only the grassy site remains. Kirkleish is shown in Ordnance Survey maps, the 1856 (1 inch to the mile) edition, and the 1908 (¹/2500 scale) edition.

Access: *OS Map Ref NX 1085 3540*

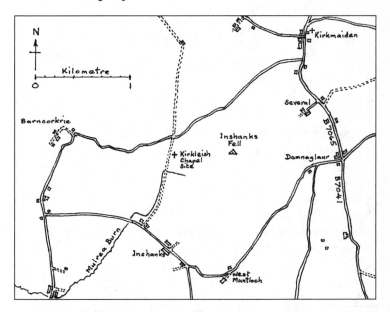

From Damnaglaur, near Drummore, proceed for 1.1 kilometre north-wards on the B7065 road, past Several Farm, then take the side road on the left westwards and south-westwards for 2.0 kilometres, until it crosses the farm-track road, which runs north to south, from Castle Clanyard to the area of Inshanks Farm. On foot, proceed southwards on this farm-track for 150 metres. On the left, eastwards into the field, at a distance of 37 metres, is the site of St Laisren's Chapel. There are no visible remains.

Kildonan Chapel,
near Drummore

In the section dealing with Chapel Donnan at Balsarroch, a little account is given of the life and death of St Donnan and of his lasting place in the Christian life of this country.

Here, in the southern Rhins, about one kilometre to the south-west of Drummore and about three-quarters of a kilometre north of Damnaglaur, on the east side of the B7065 road, there is the site of Kildonan. Here there was another little chapel — one of three in the Rhins — dedicated to St Donnan. Its date of erection is uncertain, but probably between the 7th and 11th centuries and of Celtic origin.

There are no extant remains of Kildonan Chapel.

In the first edition of the Ordnance Survey map of the Rhins area, 'Stone Ford' is clearly marked at reference point NX 1253 3613. In the Wigtownshire Name Book, No. 86, 1848, (held at the Scottish Record Office) which is a compilation of local details and anecdotal records made by Ordnance Survey personnel prior to their first edition maps, Stone Ford is described as:

> a ford crossing a stream called Kildonan Burn. It is said the ford took its name from a stone house being near it at a period when very few stone buildings were in existence in the country. This stone house was probably an old kirk which it is said stood about 5½ chains (110 metres) north of it or some other house connected therewith. No trace of them now can be found, though there are several modern houses near it.

Referring to the nearby Kildonan Hill, the same source states:

> In a field on the west side of this hill stone graves have been met with. It is said that formerly a Ch. and graveyard stood here but no trace of it can be seen now. The field has been in cultivation during the memory of the oldest inhabitant.

Nowadays, the Stone Ford is elevated about one metre above the level of the Kildonan Burn and is integral with the farm track leading to High Kildonan. A conduit allows the burn to flow under the farm track.

The Name Book information locates the old Kildonan Chapel some 60 metres north-north-east further into the field than the position given in the 1908 Ordnance Survey map (scale ½500). Since

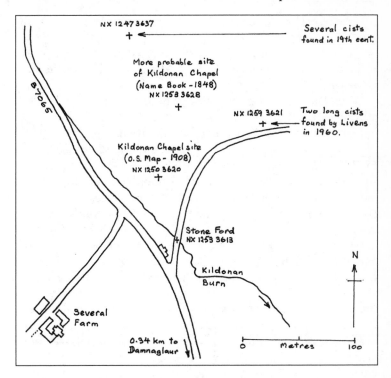

the chapel would have an adjacent burial ground, then its location would be expected to be near where cists or graves have been discovered. This expectation is satisfied by the position given for the chapel in the Name Book, *viz.* 110 metres north of Stone Ford, rather than by the position indicated in the Ordnance Survey 1908 edition map. Further, if one of these locations indicates the chapel and the other some associated residence, then it would be more appropriate for the residence rather than the chapel to be near the water source provided by the Kildonan Burn. In this light the best estimate for the position of the chapel, north of Stone Ford, is at Ordnance Survey map reference point NX 1253 3628.

Kildonan does not appear in the Timothy Pont based map of 1654. It is denoted in Robert Morden's map of 1687. Whether at this time it was in a state of decay or even ruinous is not known. The site is located in the Ordnance Survey Map, Wigtown XXXIII SW (1908).

In the New Statistical Account of Scotland in 1841 (L, 199), Kildonnan is listed as a pre-Reformation place of worship.

Todd (F, 54) lists Kildonnan as one of the six main old kirks in this southern part of the Rhins.

McKerlie (H, II, 159), in 1877, writes: 'At Kildonan no remains of a religious building are to be found, but that a chapel did stand there is to be believed.'

Scott (Y, II, 340), too, mentions the existence of a St Donan's chapel at Kildonan.

MacQueen (Q2, 31) states that the southern Rhins medieval barony of the Edgars was centred at Drummore and was succeeded by that of the Gordons which extended further south. 'The Edgars' church was probably Kildonan, and that of the Gordons Kirkmaiden.' The old Drummore barony was within the parish of Kirkmaiden, and Kildonan chapel probably functioned as a chapel-of-ease for the parish.

In the village of Drummore, in Mill Street, almost opposite the end of Stair Street, there stood a corn mill. About the year 1860, Dr (afterwards Sir) Arthur Mitchell discovered, built into the wall of the mill, a rough, undressed, engraved stone. It was described as a water-worn boulder of greywacke of irregular outline, 0.89 metre in height, 0.46 metre wide and 0.15 metre thick. The two faces of the stone were incised with rough crosses. The more elaborately sculptured face had five inset circles superimposed at the centre of the main cross; there were three other small crosses, one in the middle of the top arm of the main cross and one on each side of the bottom arm. Above the small cross at the bottom on the right was a rectangular figure, like a Roman numeral 3 or perhaps a capital letter M.

Dr Mitchell, in recording the find, states that Mr William Todd, an old gentleman (indeed, in 1860, he was in his 86th year, having retired as schoolmaster in 1843), who resided at Drummore, informed him

> that this stone had been built into the wall of a mill older than the one now existing; that still further back it had been built into the wall of the old Parish Church, and that in his young days it was held in a superstitious veneration.

McKerlie (H, II, 142) writes about this stone,

> It is said to have been brought from a chapel at Kildonan, thence removed, and built into the castle at Low Drumore, and when it became dilapidated, again removed to Drumore village, and placed in the mill wall.

Front   *Back*

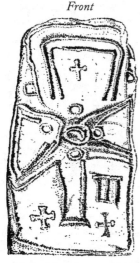

Cross-slab (c. 6th–8th century) from Drummore, now in the National Museum of Antiquities of Scotland, Edinburgh.

This early Christian stone, probably of 6th-8th century date, was given in 1874 to the National Museum of Antiquities of Scotland (IB, 33) in Edinburgh, in whose care it remains.

Up to and through the medieval period, the parish church for this area was the old Kirkmaiden Church, situated towards the Mull of Galloway. Nearer to Drummore there was Kildonan, a local chapel. Although McKerlie (1877) states that the ancient cross-inscribed stone came from Kildonan, other, perhaps more qualified, authorities such as the Royal Commission on the Ancient Historical Monuments of Scotland, simply state that it is said to have come either from the old Kirkmaiden Church or from the chapel at Kildonan. This leaves room for the speculation that if this stone came originally from the old Kirkmaiden parish church, near the Mull of Galloway Farm, then the interpreted M symbol on the stone may be for Medana. Could it be a commemorative burial stone for that 8th century local saint, from whose name the title of the parish church is derived? This may explain why, even up to the late 18th century, the stone was held in such veneration by the local people, as related, on the basis of his own experience, by Mr William Todd in 1860.

The churchyard area around Kildonan Chapel in all probability would have been a burial ground. In the 19th century, several cists were found 300 metres NNE of Several steading (c, 12). In 1960, excavation by Livens recovered an inhumation from one of two long cists revealed by ploughing in the field 260 metres NE of Several Farm steading (ibid 29). These cists would be about 120 metres NNW of Kildonan chapel site. This may simply indicate the siting of a Christian chapel on a former pagan site. It may even be the case that a Gaelic name for this site was Christianised. Todd (F, 92/93) says that Kildonnan is from the Gaelic *Cil-Dunan*, meaning 'burying place of the little hill'. The similarity of Donnan, or Dounan, the saint's name and the Gaelic word *Dunan* for a small hill, which is nearby, leaves conjecture for this identification. The association may simply be coincidental. Two hills in the area retain this linkage. Between Drummore and the chapel site there is Kildonan Hill; and on the west side of the B7065 road, between Several Farm and Damnaglaur, there is the hill named Slewdonan. In addition there is the Kildonan Burn and Kildonan Glen in the area of the chapel site.

Access: *OS Map Ref NX 1253 3628*

There are no extant remains, and at present the site is not sign-posted. One way to reach the chapel site is to proceed northwards from Damnaglaur for about 0.75 kilometre on the B7065 road. On the right-hand (east) side of the road, just before Several Cottage, there is a farm-track (unsuitable for cars) which leads up to High Kildonan. This track crosses the Kildonan Burn at a point called Stone Ford. About 110 metres north of this crossing, in a field, is the approximate position of the former Kildonan Chapel.

St Eochod's (or St Skiach's) Chapel, Hallyholm/Kilstay

Kilstay Cottage. The former chapel stood at the left of this area, near the winding track leading to the cottage.

This chapel was situated on land known as Kirk Fey. The location is about 350 metres inland from Kilstay Bay, just less than 2 kilometres north-west of Drummore. An official report (c, 27) gives the Ordnance Survey map reference as NX 125 381. This same body cites a more accurate reference as NX 1259 3817, which locates the chapel site in the Kirk Fey field, more or less on a line between Hallyholm Farm and the old Kilstay Farm building, and some 150 metres from the former and about 30 metres from the latter.

McKerlie (H, II, 151) says that Kilstay is probably from the Gaelic *Coille*, meaning a wood, and the Norse *Stia*, meaning a sheep pen, or a corruption of *Steinn*, meaning a stone. (Nearby is a standing stone site). Todd (F, 92/93), on the other hand, gives the derivation of Kilstay from *Cil-Steigh*, meaning kirk or chapel or burying place of foundation. Todd's derivation seems to come nearer to what is known about the place. He adds that this chapel was one of the six main old kirks located in this southern area of the Rhins (ibid, 54). In the New Statistical Account of Scotland in 1841 (L, 199) Kilstay is also listed as a pre-Reformation place of worship.

The word or title 'Fey' is of interest here. This term is also connected with the land just north of Balcarry on the east side of Luce Bay, where there is an old burial ground, and where formerly there was a chapel dedicated to Our Lady. The word 'Fey' seems to be connected with a person fated to die soon, with the anxious or heightened state of such a person's mind. It can also refer to something strange or other-worldly, elfin, or the little people. From these connotations it is not easy to derive the original meaning of the title 'Kirk Fey'. But there is some evidence for linking the kirk or chapel with a burial ground. It is reported that in 1848 a cist, a burial area, was located on the north side of the Pulwhinrick Burn, some 55 metres west-south-west of Kilstay Cottage. Nothing is visible of this today. Other cists are recorded and graves were found in a field to the north (c, 11). In the same report it is stated that in the 19th century many bones were ploughed up in the Kirk Fey field (ibid, 27). The 2nd edition of the Ordnance Survey 6-inch map (Wigtown, 1896, Sheet 33), also records that cists were found in an area now occupied by a disused quarry 50 metres south-south-west of Kilstay Cottage.

Interestingly, near Low Curghie, about 0.5 kilometre south-east of this chapel site, a gravestone was discovered shortly before 1860. It had a badly weathered Latin inscription, possibly dating to the 5th or 6th century. The name Ventidius was legible along with one other word given in translation as 'sub-deacon' — perhaps the Latin 'diaconus'. The use of the stone as a grave cover may suggest that it may not have been in its original position. The stone has since been lost (c, 29).

The chapel and a burial ground are reported as having been situated in the Kirk Fey field about 150 metres south-south-west of Kilstay Cottage (ibid, 27). This description positions the chapel on the south side of the present road, in a little lower neck of gently sloping farmland, bounded north and east by the Pulwhinrick Burn. In the same report, the map reference given for the chapel and burial ground is NX125 381; this situates it just on the north side of the road, within the southern part of Kirk Fey field. When this discrepancy was discussed with the member of staff who carried out the survey for the Royal Commission on the Ancient and Historical Monuments of Scotland in June 1984, he confirmed the location of the chapel site as on the north side of the road and at the southern end of the Kirk Fey field. He said that the distance given in the report as 150 metres south-south-west of Kilstay Cottage was erroneously overstated. With this clarification and the more precise map reference as NX 1259 3817, the assessed location of the chapel site is north of the present roadway, in the southern end of the Kirk Fey field, more or less on a line between Hallyholm Farm and old Kilstay Farm, and some 150 metres from the former and about 30 metres from the latter. Thus its location is quite close to some burial cists previously found, and it lies within the southern end of the Kirk Fey field in which so many bones were ploughed up in the 19th century. This fits in with the chapel having an adjacent burial ground.

It is informative to note that this secondary road beside the Pulwhinrick Burn did not exist before 1850. It is not shown on the Ordnance Survey map of that year. Instead, at that time, a lesser road ran roughly westwards from the north side of the Kilstay Bridge on the A716 road. From this lesser road a farm road led south to Kilstay, a very little further way along another farm road led north to Haly Holm, and still further on another farm road led north-westwards to Core Hill Farm on White Hill. In the Ordnance Survey map of 1895 this lesser road has disappeared and the present secondary road by the Pulwhinrick Burn has replaced it. It was after this date that Haly Holm farm was moved from its location north of Kilstay, and north of the former parallel lesser road, to its present location roughly south-south-east of Kilstay.

The chapel which formerly stood in the Kilstay-Hallyholm area is said to have been dedicated to St Skiach or St Echoid (ibid, 27). Scott (Y, II, 340) also records the existence of this chapel and says it 'appears to have been dedicated to St Skiach.' No reference can be found for a saint named Skiach. The alternative St Echoid is not listed as such, but as St Eochod (I, 186). This latter saint was one of St Columba's twelve chosen companions, who journeyed with him to Iona. He shared in the missionary work that St Columba initiated throughout Scotland. St Eochod is called the apostle of the Picts of Galloway. To have a local chapel dedicated to him would therefore not be unexpected nor inappropriate. St Eochod died in the year AD 597. The chapel at Kilstay could therefore date from as early as the 7th century.

If, on the other hand, we accept that the chapel was dedicated to St Skiach, the first difficulty is that no such named saint is found in any of the calendars. If Skiach is a derived name, then it may be related to one of the following saints.

St Kellach (Ceallach) of the 6th century, who was a disciple of St Kieran of Clonmacnoise, and who became bishop of Killalla. He ended his life as a hermit, and by some accounts as a martyr. There are several other saints of the same name (ibid, 117).

St Ceollach of the 7th century, who was an Irish prelate and for a short time governed as bishop of the Mercians or Mid-Angles. He then retired to Iona, but returned to die in his native country (ibid, 119).

St Celloch (Mochelloc, Cellog, Mottelog, Motalogus), who died *c.* 639. He is the patron saint of Kilmallock in Limerick. Authentic particulars of his life are lacking (ibid, 404).

St Keilach (Cellach, Ceilach) of the 9th century, who was archbishop of Armagh, possibly before his ordination as abbot of Iona and founder of the abbey of Kells. Colgan enumerates no less than thirty-three Celtic saints named Cellach. Most of them are evidently the same person (ibid, 119).

St Cellach (Celsus) who died in 1129. He was Cellach McAedh, a native of Ireland, who seems to have been a Benedictine monk at Glastonbury. He certainly was for a time at Oxford, and in 1106 was ordained archbishop of Armagh. He proved to be a great prelate and a restorer of church discipline throughout Ireland. When dying he sent his pastoral staff to St Malachy, then bishop of Connor, who became his successor. He was the last hereditary archbishop of Armagh (ibid, 119).

St Canice, otherwise known as Canicus, Cainnech, Kenny and Kenneth. He lived from *c.* 525 to *c.* 599. Born in Northern Ireland, he was trained to the monastic life under St Finian of Clonard, and St Cadoc in Wales. Then he went to Glasnevin. He founded the monastery of Agahanoe and perhaps of Kilkenny, and later preached in Scotland under St Columba and was the first to build a church in the place now known as St Andrews. The city of Kilkenny is named after him (ibid, 109).

Access: *OS Map Ref NX 1259 3817*

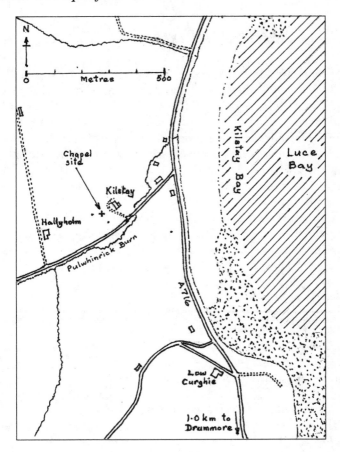

The turning to Hallyholm is off the A716 road, just under 2.0 kilometres north of Drummore. There are no remains of the chapel.

St Bride's Chapel, Kirkbride

About five kilometres north of Drummore, just inland from Terally Bay, there are the ruined remains of a Celtic chapel dedicated to St Brigid. In the section dealing with the other Kirkbryde site, in the North Rhins, an account is given of this Irish saint's life. The Celtic monks and missionaries brought her fame with them and inserted it into our heritage through the many places and churches named in her honour and under her patronage. And so we have two such chapels, one in the North and this one in the South Rhins.

This southern Rhins chapel at Kirkbride was built probably between the 7th and the 14th centuries. MacQueen (Q2, 20) says that it seems to be the ruins of a small medieval chapel. He adds (ibid, 25) that it might date from any period of the Middle Ages. He also notes (ibid, 31) that it lay within the parish of Kirkmaiden, and thus it would be used as a chapel-of-ease and be served by a priest from Kirkmaiden parish church. There are no old records or references to throw more light on its origin or history.

Kirkbride is not shown in the Pont-Blaeu map of 1654. In General William Roy's map of c. 1747 he records it as Killbryde. John Ainslie carried out a survey of the Rhins area in 1781. In his beautifully detailed map of 1782 he records 'Kirkbride ruins' and locates them to the east of Killumpha. The latter farm still exists.

In the new Statistical Account of Scotland in 1841 (L, 199), Kirkbride is listed as a pre-Reformation place of worship.

Todd (F, 54/55) includes Kirkbride as one of six ancient Kirks in this South Rhins area, and adds that it appears to be one of the last to be built. He goes on to say, writing in 1854, that 'at Kirkbride, the foundations are in a great measure undisturbed and the ruins unremoved.'

Scott (Y, II, 340), too, mentions the existence of St Bride's Chapel at Kirkbride.

The chapel ruins stand on a gentle hillside, with a fine view eastwards of Luce Bay and the Machars peninsula. Within a kilometre radius of the site lie three farms: westwards, Killumpha; eastwards, Terally; and south-westwards, Kirkbride.

Though no chapel walls are still standing, the foundations of the walls and remaining fallen stones, partly covered with soil and shrubbery, still provide some evidence of the configuration of the chapel. It was of rectangular shape and lay on an east-west axis, like most early church buildings.

A fairly common feature found in many early Western European church buildings is their east-west longitudinal axis. There is a tradition saying that thus they pointed in the direction of the Holy Land. So many old abbey churches, cathedrals, and early parish churches and chapels conform to this pattern. These usually have the main entrance at the west end and the high altar at the east end of the nave. This is the arrangement with nearly all the ancient churches and chapels of the Rhins. Kirkbride chapel, too, shares this east-west configuration of its main axis.

The rectangular dimensions of this Chapel of St Bride (Brigid) are approximately 14.0 metres by 3.7 metres. Other foundational stone remains in the north-east corner and the west end indicate either adjoining parts to the chapel or enclosure walls.

An official report (c, 36) about Kirkbride in 1984 describes it as follows:

> Situated in an area of unimproved ground 400 metres north-east of Kirkbride farmhouse, there are the remains of a roughly oval enclosure measuring 27 metres by 25 metres within an earth-and-stone bank up to 8.5 metres thick and 1.5 metres high. The east side of the enclosure is overlain by a three-compartment rectangular building measuring 14 metres by 3.7 metres within stone walls 1.1 metre thick and 0.6 metre high; banks radiating from the north-west and south-west corners of the building divide the enclosure into three courts. Two further enclosures on the east measure 16.3 metres by 6.2 metres and 12 metres by 9.4 metres respectively within banks 1.2 metres thick and 0.3 metre high. Although the remains are said to be those of a church dedicated to St Bride, they appear to be of a secular character.

A rath is a circular earthwork, providing defence for a homestead or settlement. Sir Andrew Agnew (w, 178) states that a bygone chapel at Topmalloch on his Lochnaw estate had no rath. It would seem that a few church buildings had such protective surroundings. Here at Kirkbride the remains of a rath are evident. Similarly there are considerable earthworks surrounding the medieval site of Inch parish church. At Kirkbride there may be a question as to whether or not the church was built within an existing rath, one that may have served some earlier purpose.

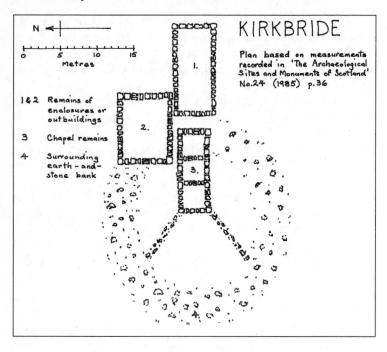

N

0   5   10   15
Metres

KIRKBRIDE

Plan based on measurements
recorded in 'The Archaeological
Sites and Monuments of Scotland'
No.24 (1985) p.36

1 & 2   Remains of
         enclosures or
         outbuildings

3   Chapel remains

4   Surrounding
         earth - and -
         stone bank

Though there is no superficial evidence, it would be most probable that the churchyard area would serve as a burial-ground.

Sometimes in the past a Christian centre would be established to replace a preceding pagan one. This may apply to the siting of St Bride's Chapel.

As already mentioned, there are three farms not far distant from the chapel site — Killumpha, Terally and Kirkbride. Todd (F, 49), in 1854, says that the latter two were 'not very long since parts of the same farm.' Some corroboration for this may be gleaned from Ainslie's 1782 map of the area, which indicates only the farms of Killumpha and Tyrawley, and, with a little church symbol, indicates 'Kirkbride ruins'.

In 1955 eleven long burial cists were found by workmen digging a trench along the edge of the raised beach to the north of Terally Bridge. In 1956 excavation by Livens revealed a further two cists and showed that the cemetery was bounded on the north by a standing stone (which is still to be seen, about 700 metres north of Terally farm) and on the south by a natural mound known as Terally Mote. The graves were probably all aligned east-west and contained extended inhumations. Numerous flint flakes, some worked, and all probably of Mesolithic date, were found during the excavations. (c, 30)

Todd (F, 49) refers to the standing stone as a very ancient grave-stone and offers a conjecture that it may mark the spot where a Druid of the order of Fay or prophet may have been buried, and from this may have been derived the name Killumpha, taken from Kil-am-fay, a corruption of the Gaelic *Cil-am-faidh*, the grave of the prophet or fay, i.e. soothsayer.

So the pagan Druid associations with this area may have prompted the Christian siting and erection of St Bride's Chapel in this vicinity.

Notwithstanding Todd's derivation, MacQueen (Q2, 20) says that Killumpha is interpreted as 'Iomchadh's church' — a commemoration of a very obscure saint.

Access: *OS Map Ref NX 1194 4042*

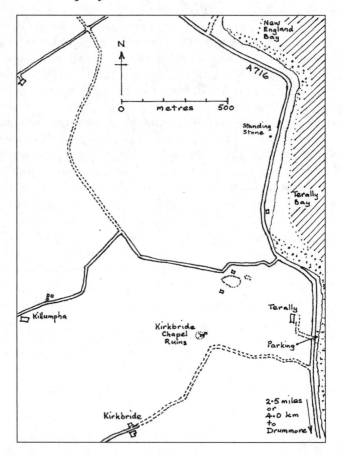

The site is presently not signposted. Cars are probably best parked somewhere off the main A716 road just south of Terally Farm, some 4 kilometres north of Drummore. Walk up the Kirkbride farm track for some 400 metres, then north-west, in the field to the right, at a distance of about 100 metres are the ruined remains of Kirkbride Chapel. The site is situated on private farmland.

St Ninian's Chapel, Chipperdingan

A chapel dedicated to St Ninian is said to have stood on the north-west side of Myroch Hill, inland from New England Bay in the southern Rhins (c, 26).

It is mentioned by Scott (Y, II, 340) that a St Ninian's Chapel stood at Chipperdingan; and perhaps by way of explaining the derivation of the place-name, he adds that Tobar Niniain equates to St Ninian's Well. MacQueen (Q2, 20), with his Gaelic expertise, states that Chipperdingan means 'thy Finnian's well' and that this is to be associated with St Finian's Chapel, which stood at Killingeane, just north of the location of the well.

There seems no substantial evidence nor other reporting of the existence of this chapel dedicated to St Ninian, apart from a mention in the Name Book, Wigtown, No. 81, p.21.

With such obscurity of information, very little can be discerned about this particular chapel. Its rough location is given by the map reference below, supplied by the Royal Commission on the Ancient Historical Monuments of Scotland (c, 26).

Access: *OS Map Ref NX 11 41*

The site is not located with precision. It lies roughly inland from New England Bay, somewhere on the north-west side of Myroch Hill. There is a car park at New England Bay, just off the A716 road, about 5.5 kilometres north of Drummore.

St Finian's Chapel, Killingeane

This chapel dedicated to St Finian may have served as a chapel-of-ease for the barony of Logan (cf. Q2, 31). It is said to have stood at Killingeane (c, 27). This location is about 100 metres east of the A716 road and some 400 metres north of the junction of the A716 and B7065 roads. There are no remains to be seen.

There is a companion chapel dedicated to St Finian across Luce Bay on the west coast of the Machars. St Finian had links with this area, and so it is not unexpected to find churches or chapels dedicated to him.

There are at least three St Finians — all Irish. The one connected with this part of Scotland is St Finian of Moville. He was born near Strangford Lough in *c.* 493. After some education in Ireland under St Colman, he came across the Irish Sea to Whithorn, at which place St Ninian had established the first diocesan church and community in *c.* 397. Having spent some time at Whithorn as a monk, St Finian is said to have gone to Rome, where he was ordained priest, and returned to Ireland. He established a monastery at Moville (Maghbile) in County Down, which became an Irish centre of learning. It was there that St Columba was a disciple of St Finian. St Columba came to Scotland in 563, established his community at Iona and was instrumental in the evangelisation and conversion to Christianity of the northern half of Scotland and of sustaining St Ninian's earlier work in the south of the country. St Finian therefore was an influential figure in the early life of the Church in Scotland, being a kind of link between Whithorn and Iona. He died about the year 579.

So, St Finian's Chapel at Killingeane in the Rhins would be Celtic-inspired and could date from as early as the 6th or 7th century. MacQueen (Q2, 25) supports this early foundation dating for this chapel. If the chapel existed from such early times, it seems through the medieval period to have come under the patronage of the barony of Logan and served the local populace as a chapel-of-ease. This can be understood with the awareness that its location is between the two relatively distant medieval parish churches of Kirkmadrine to the north and Kirkmaiden to the south.

South-east and very close to the chapel site is a little hill named Knocktaggart (OS Map Ref NX 1090 4375). McKerlie (H, II, 173) says:

> Todd in his manuscript (1854) derives Knocktaggart from the Gaelic *Cnoc-t-sagairt*, the priests' hill. We find in the Gaelic, *tagairt*, a pleading, from *tagair* to plead. In *Cnoc* we have an eminence or hill, and the compound word seems to us to point to a preacher or lawgiver.

Scott (Y, II, 340) states *Cnoc an t-sagairt* means the Priest's Hill.

MacQueen (Q2, 20) states that Chipperdingan (thy Finian's well), the location of which is just south of the site of Killingeane, is to be associated with St Finian's Chapel.

Access: *OS Map Ref NX 108 438*

The site, without remains, is on the east side of the A716 Drummore road, about 400 metres north of its junction with the B7065 road. The given location is about 100 metres east of the main road on the north-west side of the hill.

Kirkholm Chapel

The word 'holm' may describe a piece of flat ground by a river, which is submerged in time of flood. The word seems to be derived from the Old Norse word *holmr*. This may indicate that the chapel followed the Viking period, and probably dates from between the late 9th to the 12th centuries. In Ainslie's 1782 map of the area he indicates a moss or boggy area about 1.0 kilometre north of Logan House. The 1986 Ordnance Survey map describes this same location as Logan Moss. The area is now a non-coniferous wood, which straddles a little stream that has its origin slightly south-west of Logan Moss and 0.6 kilometre south of Drumbreddan Farm; 0.25 kilometre south of the same farm is Kirkholm Hill. Approximately halfway between the summit of this hill and the little stream to the south is the site of the ancient Kirkholm Chapel (c, 27). There are no visible remains. The maps of Blaeu/Pont 1654, Roy *c*. 1747, and Ainslie 1782, do not indicate this chapel. This could be because of its smallness or perhaps, more likely, its ruination and disappearance. If the chapel survived to the Reformation in 1560, then it does not appear to have survived much beyond that date.

Access: *OS Map Ref NX 084 436*

From the village of Ardwell take the Clachanmore road. Pass Ardwell Church, then take the first turning to the left (south), going via Cairnhandy to Drumbreddan Farm. The site, with no remains, is 0.5 kilometre south of the farm, between the bottom of the hill and the stream.

Chapel Rossan

In 1839, the Rev John Lamb reporting on Kirkmaiden parish states:
The public road enters at the north-east corner, at a small modern building of antique construction, erected as a porter's lodge, or to commemorate the name of a place where, in old times, stood a kirk or chapel called Chapelrossan, or the chapel of the promontory.' (L, 200)

McKerlie (H, II, 141) writes 'Chapelrossan, that is the chapel at the promontory, of which nothing is known…'. This chapel was located on a little headland jutting eastwards, south of Ardwell, in what is now called Chapel Rossan Bay. McKerlie in referring to Chapel Rossan as 'the chapel at the promontory' accepts the geographical derivation from the word ross (Gaelic *ros*, meaning a promontory). Alternatively, it is said that Chapel Rossan is a title derived from St Drostan to whom the chapel was dedicated (c, 26).

Scott (Y, II, 340) states that there was a St Drostan's Chapel at Chapel Rossan.

St Drostan, an Irishman by birth, was a monk under St Columba. When a foundation was made at Deer in Aberdeenshire, St Drostan was appointed its first abbot. He is venerated as one of the apostles of Scotland. A holy well near Aberdour is named after him. After his death, *c.* 610, he was buried at Aberdour (J, III, 71).

The St Drostan dedication for this chapel would suggest its establishment within the Celtic period from the 7th to the 11th centuries. Although nothing is known of its subsequent history, Chapel Rossan is referred to in later maps. It is not mentioned in the map of Blaeu/Pont in 1654 — the map scale does not perhaps allow for details other than large buildings, more prominent churches, and villages. However, in the Roy map, *c.* 1747, a building is shown on the promontory and is referred to as Chapel Rossan. In the Ainslie map of 1782, Chapel Rossan is denoted by a small group of buildings in the south-west corner of Chapel Rossan Bay. Today, there are no visible remains of the ancient chapel.

Access: *OS Map Ref NX 1090 4505*

The location given is in the south-western part of Chapel Rossan Bay, just off the A716 road, just south of Ardwell Village.

Killaser

Only Scott states that a chapel existed at this site. In 1917 (Y, II, 353) his publication states that there was a St Lashrean's Chapel at Killaser, within the parish of Stoneykirk. In 1950 (Y, VIII, 191) the same source states that the church was dedicated to St Lassair (Laisre, Lasrach, Lassar). Such unexplained contradiction in the matter of dedication, added to the absence of claim or evidence from any other source, leaves a large measure of uncertainty and questions the authenticity of the claim as to the very existence of such a chapel.

The name Killaser survives only in reference to the remains of a castle. It belonged to the McCullochs of Ardwell (E, 149).

> The remains of this tower-house stand within the vestiges of a ditched enclosure in an area of low-lying ground 440 metres south-east of Cairnhandy farmhouse. The rectangular tower (6.5 metres by 4.8 metres within a wall up to 2.1 metres thick) has been reduced to its lowest courses, but enough survives to indicate the presence of a vaulted ground floor, a mural passage and the possible provision for a stair or latrine at the north-east angle. (C, 33)

The small fortified house survived the chapel, if the latter existed. Only the name gives support to the existence of a chapel here. St Laisren is already commemorated in the South Rhins with a chapel at Inshanks. He probably traversed the district on his route to and from Ireland and Northumbria. St Lasar (Lassar, Lassera) was a 6th century Irish nun, a niece of St Forchera. She was in early life placed under the care of St Finian and St Kiernan at Clonard. Her name means 'Flame' (I, 336). St Finian taught St Columba, and he, through the influence of his Iona community, could have spread knowledge of her throughout Scotland. Interestingly, St Colman, to whom the church of Colmonell in Southern Ayrshire was dedicated, is said to have visited the cell of St Lassar and was also associated with St Columba (Q2, 19, 22).

The McCullochs were prominent feudal landowners and have had some reason for naming their fortified house here, Killaser. The explanation remains obscure. Apart from the castle, the existence of the chapel can only be conjectured.

McKerlie (H, II, 174) proffers an alternative explanation. He points out that Pont, the 16th-17th century surveyor-mapmaker, spells Killaster as Killaister. McKerlie says:

> In the Gaelic there are the words *Kil* and *Astar*, but the latter (meaning a journey or distance) cannot apply here. There is also *Aisre* and *Aisridh*, an abode, which with *Kil* as a corruption of the Gaelic for a wood, may give the meaning.

Access: *OS Map Ref NX 0964 4509*

About 700 metres southwards along the lesser road from Ardwell Church, the castle ruins lie a short distance to the west.

Kirkmabreck

Achapel dedicated to St Brioch is said to have stood at Kirkmabreck (Y, II, 353), (C, 28). The present farm of Kirkmabreck is situated about 1.5 kilometres south of Sandhead. Roy, in his map *c.* 1747, does not use special symbols for churches, but indicates Kirk McBreck. Ainslie in his 1782 map, shows, in close proximity, an East, West and North Kirkmabreck and a Kirkmabreck Mill. His North Kirkmabreck seems to be the location of the present Kirkmabreck Farm (OS Map Ref NX 099 480) and the probable site of St Brioch's Chapel.

The 'ma' in Kirkmabreck is very likely derived from the Irish-Gaelic *mo*, being an honorific prefix of endearment. But the dedication of this chapel poses a problem since there is no Saint Breck or Saint Brioch mentioned in any of the calendar sources. Light falls on six possibilities:

1. St Brioc (Brieuc, Briocus), *c.* 420-510, who was born in Dyfed, Wales, and educated in France by St Germanus of Auxerre. He then laboured successfully in Wales and then in Brittany, where he founded two abbeys, one near Treguier, the other in the town of St Brieuc, named after him.

2. St Breaca (Breague, Branca, Banka), 5th-6th century, who was a disciple of St Brigid in Ireland, then went to Cornwall (*c.* 460) with several companions.

3. St Brice (Britius, Brixius, Brictio), who died in 444. He was a trouble-some disciple of St Martin of Tours, (to whom Whithorn, Kirkmadrine, and many other churches were dedicated). Nevertheless he was chosen to succeed St Martin in 397, and was an unsatisfactory bishop for some twenty years. Having incurred ignominy, he went to Rome, reformed, cleared his name, returned to Tours and continued as a very commendable bishop, being popularly proclaimed a saint immediately after his death. His cult extended to Britain.

4. St Rioch, who died *c.* 480. He is described as a nephew of St Patrick, and may have come to Whithorn for spiritual learning. Very little is known about him, but he followed a religious life and was the abbot of Innisboffin, in Ireland.

5. McKerlie (H, II, 140) says that this chapel was dedicated to St Bridgit. An account of St Bridgit (Bride) is given in the section dealing with Kirkbryde in the North Rhins.

6. MacQueen (Q2, 21) says Kirkmabreck is 'Church of Mo-Bhric', or just possibly 'Church of Aedh mac Bric'. The latter is listed (1, 10) under Aedh MacBrice, an Irish saint of the 6th century. The name is also spelt Aod and Aedsind, and it is Latinised as Aidus. He was a disciple of St Illadan at Rathlihen in Offaly, and is said to have founded churches at Rathugh and other places in his native Meath, where he held the office of bishop.

The supposition is that the chapel at Kirkmabreck would be a Celtic foundation, probably dating in origin from about the 7th to the 12th century. There are no remains, but the name is perpetuated in the place name.

Access: *OS Map Ref NX c09 48*

The farm of Kirkmabreck lies to the west of the A716 road, a short distance south of the turn off for Kirkmadrine and Clachanmore.

Kirkmagill

Balgreggan Mains, with wooded knoll of Molly's Grove to the left.

A little more than one kilometre west of Sandhead lies Balgreggan Mains. Adjacent and westwards of the house is a wooded knoll, sometimes known as Molly's Grove. This is the site of a Celtic or early medieval chapel referred to as Kirkmagill.

This chapel may have been dedicated to St Maughold (also known as Maccul, or Maccaldus or Machalus or MacCaille), an Irishman said to have been a brigand, but converted by St Patrick and sent by him to the Isle of Man, where as bishop he was very successful. He died *c.* 488.

Another saint to whom the chapel may have been dedicated is St Maguil (or Mauguille; also known as Madelgisilus). He was an Irish monk, a disciple and trusted confidant of St Fursey. After some years of monastic life at St Riquier, he retired, together with his friend St Pulgan (or Vulgan), to a solitude near Monstrelet, where he died *c.* 655.

P H McKerlie (H, II, 158) writes: 'The suffix gill might also be assumed to be the Gaelic gil from geal, meaning white, and thus from the appearance of the stone named the white chapel.'

If Kirkmagill was dedicated to St Maughold, then this would be influenced by the nearness of the Rhins to the Isle of Man, and the probable ease with which the cult of this saintly bishop spread across the Irish Sea. Another possible link with St Maughold (or MacCaille) is that his life overlapped that of St Brigid (or Bride). One source (J, I, 226) states that she was 'veiled' for the religious life by St MacCaille at Mag Teloch in Ireland. Not far from Kirkmagill in the southern Rhins, some 10 kilometres further south, between Terally and Kirkbride Farms, there are the ruins of a Celtic chapel dedicated to St Brigid (Bride). The proximity of these two chapels to each other may be coincidental or may be an indication of a traditional link between these two saints. St Brigid, of course, is the more widely known of the two.

On the other hand, if the chapel was dedicated to St Maguil, whose religious life was centred in France, it might suggest a 7th- or 8th-century foundation for Kirkmagill, perhaps soon after the saint's death.

It is not possible to be more precise than to suggest that the chapel at Kirkmagill was erected sometime between the 7th and the 12th centuries. It may have had some connection, even patronage, from the succession of McDowalls, historic landowners in these parts, whose residence was at Balgreggan.

MacQueen (Q2, 30) writes:

> The older name for Sandhead on Luce Bay was Balgreggan (baile, 'steading'; and probably gragan, 'manor, big house'). The modern village street is clearly aligned on an impressive Norman motte or castle hill, still called the Motte of Balgreggan, and the gragan which gave the village its name was, I suggest, either the wooden castle which once crowned the motte hill, or the tower house which probably succeeded it, and stood on the site of the modern Balgreggan House. The name Balgreggan, that is to say, cannot have come into existence much before the end of the 12th century, and may even be considerably later. Balgreggan is one of several Gaelic-speaking villages whch grew up in the shadow of a Norman motte.

It is noteworthy that in the Pont-Blaeu map of 1654 Balgreggan is indicated, not Sandhead. In Roy's map of *c.* 1747 the Mote of Balgregan and Castle McDougal [McDowall] are indicated, and Sandhead is titled Sandy Croft.

With permission of the owner, an inspection of the Kirkmagill site in January 1995 revealed foundational remains of a wall at the location of the chapel. Apart from this, there are no remains above ground level.

The fenced and walled enclosure around this wooded knoll site of the chapel may indicate the extent of its churchyard. This is likely also to be a burial ground.

It would seem that the chapel existed at the time of the Reformation, in 1560, and beyond.

Timothy Pont, who did map-survey work in Galloway *c.* 1595, has recorded a Kirmagill in his map.

General William Roy's map of *c.* 1747 records Kirk McGill.

P H McKerlie (H, II, 158), writing in 1877, reports no building on the site.

The Ordnance Survey (½2500 scale) map of 1908 locates the site of Kirkmagill in the centre of the wooded knoll, known as Molly's Grove.

Access: *OS Map Ref NX 0850 5023*

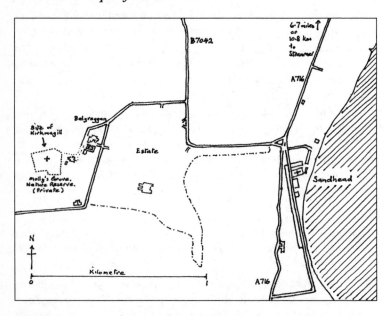

The present owner, resident at Balgreggan Mains, maintains the wooded knoll of Molly's Grove as a nature reserve. This site of Kirkmagill is therefore at present not generally made available to the public.

Kirklauchline

The title of this farm may suggest that a chapel was once on this site, but there are no references in any records of this being the case, nor is there any visible evidence. The name alone gives rise to the conjecture. Even the name is problematical. It implies the Church or Chapel of Lauchline, but there is no record of such a named saint. The nearest saints' names to Lauchline are Luchtighern (6th century) and Laicin (7th century), both Irish.

McKerlie(H, II, 159) proffers an alternative explanation for the name Kirklauchline.

The Pont/Blaeu map of 1654 does not show Kirklauchline. But in Pont's survey, *c*. 1595, it is recorded as Kirlochlyn and also as Keirlachlyn. In Roy's map, *c*. 1747, it is shown as Kirlachlan. In Ainslie's 1782 map it is shown as Kirlauchly. Although the farm is presently called Kirklauchline, and is shown as such in the current Ordnance Survey maps, McKerlie states that since it was earlier referred to as *Kir*, which is a contraction of *caer*, from the Gaelic *cathair*, a fortress, then the farm is named from a nearby ancient fort site, overlooking Portayew Bay. The Gaelic prefix *Kir* is also used for a town or settlement. McKerlie adds that Lauchline is a corruption of the Gaelic word *Lochlin*, meaning Scandinavia (referring to Norsemen). When writing, in *c*. 1877, he says that the local people then referred to the fort site as the *Kempes*, which in the Norse means a warrior. In this way he derives the meaning of Kirklauchline as being castle or settlement of the Norsemen.

Nearness to the site of Kildonan Chapel adds weight to McKerlie's interpretation, and the unlikelihood of a chapel at Kirklauchline.

Access: *OS Map Ref NX 043 508*

This site at Kirklauchline can be reached from the B7042 road from Sandhead to the Portpatrick A77 road. To the west of Awhirk Farm follow the secondary road south for about 2.3 kilometres.

Central Rhins

Soulseat Abbey

Clayshant Parish Church

Inch Parish Church

Stoneykirk Parish Church

Chapel of St John, Stranraer

Chapel Patrick, Portpatrick

St Ninian's Chapel, Killantringan

St Catherine's Chapel, Eldrickhill

Kildonan Chapel, Near Stoneykirk

Soulseat Abbey

The double-promontory of the Rhins proper is connected to the adjacent mainland by a low neck of land. On this isthmus, some 4.5 kilometres south-east of Stranraer, is situated Soulseat Loch. This little inland loch has its own promontory, which juts into the loch from its south-west corner. This is the site of Soulseat Abbey, which in its time was a centre for the Premonstratensian Order in Scotland.

Within about a century of the Norman conquest of England in

1066, Norman lords and French-derived religious foundations began to be seen in Scotland. Cistercian, Cluniac and Premonstratensian were three such religious orders that arrived in Scotland at this time.

At the end of the 11th century there was a general wave of reform in the Church, which had a considerable impact on the ordered way of life of monks and nuns.

In Scotland, this internal Church reformation was given impetus by the good influence of St Margaret, the Queen (d. 1093). Three of her sons succeeded as Kings of Scotland; the most notable of these was King David 1 (d. 1153) who continued the general and religious renaissance throughout the country. He established five new dioceses and founded numerous monasteries, among them the Cistercian Abbey at Dundrennan.

At this time there lived St Malachy (1095-1148), a reforming Bishop of Down. It seems he made the journey, more than once, from Ireland to Rome, by way of Galloway. His life was written by his friend, St Bernard of Clairvaux. From this source it appears that St Malachy knew the site of Soulseat and intended founding a monastery there as early as 1141. Though not a monk himself, St Malachy so admired the Cistercians that he founded the first house of that Order in Ireland, at Mellifort, in 1142. According to St Bernard's *Life of St Malachy*, the latter, on a later journey, brought an abbot and monks and established them at Soulseat. They may have been Cistercians but there is no certainty that these monks were of that Order. The year is reckoned to be 1147. Whatever these facts may be, it seems from subsequent events that these monks did not continue in residence for long.

Soulseat is in the Diocese of Galloway, and from *c.* 1125 to *c.* 1154 the bishop was Gilla-Aldan. He, after the death of St Malachy, again founded Soulseat, and intended installing Augustinian Canons. Galloway at this time under the control of a native ruler, Fergus, Lord of Galloway, was merging into union with the rest of Scotland under King David 1. Gilla-Aldan, who was Fergus's Bishop, was succeeded in 1154 by Bishop Christian, who preferred Premonstratensians for Soulseat. This was an Order of Canons, founded by St Norbert in 1120 at Premontre in France. So it was that these Canons came from Premontre to Soulseat, probably between 1155 and 1160.

Cowan and Easson (B, 100) say:

The history of the houses of this order in Scotland is difficult to reconstruct as the only surviving chartulary is that of Dryburgh. The foundation of that abbey in 1150 is usually reckoned as marking the establishment of the order in Scotland, but a case can be mounted in support of Soulseat's claim to have been the first Scottish Premonstratensian house.

It was from Soulseat that both Whithorn (*c.* 1177) and Holywood (*c.* 13th century) were provided with the beginnings of their Premonstratensian communities (N, 163). Cowan and Easson (B, 101-2) indicate that Holywood was founded before 1225.

From 1177, and on through the ensuing centuries, Whithorn surpassed Soulseat in size, importance and wealth, mainly because of the many pilgrims who came to the shrine of St Ninian. King James IV was such a pilgrim and personally appealed to Rome for Whithorn's superiority over Soulseat, but the appeal was rejected. So, despite controversy, Soulseat continued to hold its principal status, and continued as a Premonstratensian abbey for four centuries, until the Reformation in the 16th century. In 1542, the Abbot of Soulseat was made Visitator of Premonstratensian Houses in Scotland by Pope Paul III.

Monasteries were not exempt from the ravages of weather, wear and wars. By the latter end of the 14th century Soulseat was in a poor state. On 15 July 1393 Pope Clement VII issued approval to Finlay, then Abbot of Soulseat, to secure annexation of the parish church of Kirkmaiden in 'le Rynnis', on the grounds that the fruits of the abbey could not sustain the abbot and community, and that, owing to wars, the abbey buildings were in a dilapidated condition. Thereafter Kirkmaiden was served by a canon of Soulseat (K, 92).

The names of only a few Canons of Soulseat survive in documents of the period. Among them, in the 15th century, are Cornelius Macmaken and Gilbert Makdonyl (ibid, 92), both of whom were vicars of the annexed Kirkmaiden parish.

As a result of Whithorn's wealthy sway, King James IV wrote in 1505 and obtained approval from the General of the Premonstratensians to make Whithorn the principal house of the order in Scotland and with full jurisdiction in visitation and reformation, all of which was then held by the abbot of Soulseat. This new power was exercised drastically by Whithorn, so the king wrote again in 1507, and was supported by the abbot of Dryburgh, to have the General rescind the authority granted to Whithorn and transfer the pre-eminence to Dryburgh. The reply is unknown. If the request was granted, then it appears that within a relatively short time it was again restored to Soulseat. In 1524, Quentin, abbot of Soulseat, is described in a Crown letter as 'father superior of the Premonstratensian order in Scotland'. Again in 1532 David, abbot of Soulseat, received Crown letters ordaining everyone in authority to assist and protect him in visiting and reforming all the houses in Scotland of the Premonstratensian order, a commission given him by the father abbot and general chapter of Premontre (ibid, 90-91) (L, 87). So despite other vying points of view and the influence of greater wealth at other houses, lowly Soulseat seems to have for the most part throughout its history retained its pre-eminence among the six Premonstratensian foundations in Scotland.

In 1504, Quintin Vaux was Abbot of Soulseat. David Vaux succeeded him as abbot. George Freebairn and Thomas Gellatly are mentioned at Soulseat in the 1540s. Two other Premonstratensian Canons of Soulseat, John White and James Thomson, survived the Reformation of 1560 (O, 59-60). The latter was reader at Soulseat during the period 1563-1574 (Z, 221).

Perhaps some further evidence of the very small number of canons at Soulseat, at the time of the Reformation, is given by a Deed, dated 27 March, 1558, which attests that Canon Frederick Bruce, who was Subprior at Whithorn, was also vicar of Soulseat Parish Church and Toskerton too (ibid, 53). It can be argued that this appointment to Soulseat was due to insufficient canons resident there to meet their internal and external commitments.

Throughout its 400-year history up to the time of the Reformation, Soulseat doubled in being both an abbey and a parish church. Cowan (A, 61) says:

> The revenues of the church, both parsonage and vicarage, pertained to the abbey of Soulseat at the Reformation, one of the canons serving the cure. These would undoubtedly appear to have been annexed at the abbey's foundation in the mid-twelfth century.

After 1532, commendators, who were religious superiors without themselves being monks or canons (sometimes they were secular priests, at other times laymen), ruled Soulseat. It was provided in commendam on 18 July, 1533, to James Johnstone, rector of Johnstone, a secular priest of the Diocese of Glasgow. In 1545 it passed to his successor John Johnstone, a fellow secular priest. He evidently signed a bond in 1568 promising to fight for Mary, Queen of Scots. Unlike so many of the prelates of the Church at the Reformation, Abbot John remained true to the ancient faith. He is notable for having been prosecuted for saying Mass after the Reformation prohibition of 1560. It was on 26 June 1572 that he was 'delaited for the administratione of the Mass and the Sacraments in the Papisticall manner.' (s, 43). The Kennedys, influenial landowners, disputed his tenure. 'He was kidnapped by the Kennedies and Adairs and tortured in the castle of Dunskey. (At this time, it is recorded that Mr James Fothinghame — minister of Glenluce — had oversight of Soulseat church in 1574 (z, 221)). But like the abbot of Crossraguel, who also suffered from the Kennedys' tortures, John Johnstone lived long enough to take action against his tormentors', and his claim to Soulseat eventually succeeded. He remained in office until 1598. 'He died in 1600, having made his testament on the 14 April. He had two illegitimate sons.' (k, 98)

The Soulseat property then passed under the control of a series of appointed laymen commendators:

Mr John Kennedy	1598
Mr John Johnston	1598/9-*c.* 1601
William Adair younger of Kinhilt	1601
Mr John Hamilton	1612-1630 (ibid, 98-9)

In 1630, the abbey lands were secularised, the abbey emoluments were transferred to the new church at Portpatrick, and the parish of Soulseat was united with Inch. According to Reid (ibid, 99), little could have remained of the abbey at that time.

Timothy Pont surveyed Galloway *c.* 1595. In the Blaeu map of 1654, resulting from Pont's work, Soulseat is described by the word 'Abbey'.

Writing in 1684 about Soulseat Abbey, Symson (G, 58) says:

> The manse belonging to the minister of Inch is seated here, though a mile distant from the kirk; and the gleib is environed with this loch, and a short trench drawn from one corner to the other thereof.

This trench or moat across the neck of the promontory is shown on Ainslie's map of 1782.

The abbey graveyard, on the mid-eastern side of the promontory, remained in use at least into the 18th century. A few of the gravestones remain today.

In 1838, a new Church of Scotland manse was built for the minister of Inch parish beside the site of the abbey at Soulseat. McKerlie (H, I, 145), writing in 1877, says:

> The manse and glebe of Inch now occupy the site of the Abbey, of which only a few vaults and other fragments remain. In trenching the ground a great many human bones have been dug up.

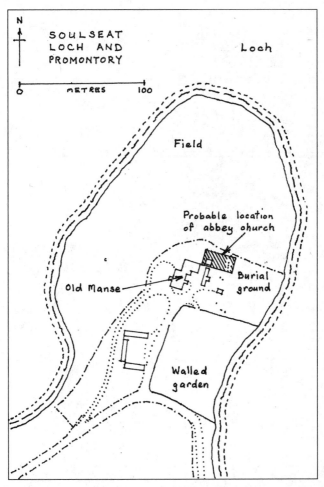

Writing about Soulseat Abbey in 1917, Scott (Y, II, 336) reports, 'The remains are now but scanty.' He adds, 'Near its ruins is St John's Croft.'

The 19th-century house is no longer used as a manse. The McKinley family took over the property in 1983 and have developed the old walled garden area as a herb garden. This property, called Meadowsweet, is open to the public in season.

Reid (K, 91), in 1960, writing about Soulseat Abbey, says:

Surface indications are of a cruciform church of normal Premonstratensian type, with transepts of two bays and an aisleless nave. It is possible that the back half of the present manse is built on the line of the west range.

Site of Soulseat Abbey

At Soulseat, in March 1986, some studies and prospective excavations were carried out by The Royal Commission on the Ancient Historical Monuments of Scotland, and the results were published in 1987. The report states:

> To the east of the manse building there are the turf-covered remains of a robbed rectangular building, aligned east to west, and measuring about 20.8 metres by 13.0 metres overall; and about 12.0 metres to the south a small area of cobbling has been revealed. Traces of a ditch (up to 6.0 metres broad and 0.2 metres deep), are visible across the neck of the promontory. On the south side of the ancient building remains there are a 17th-century grave-slab and a number of 18th-century gravestones. (D, 61)

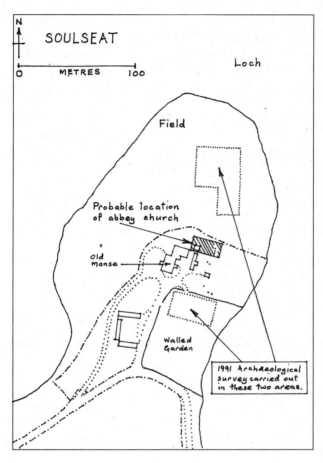

These confirmatory findings help to locate more precisely the abbey church remains, situated immediately on the east side of the existing 19th century manse, and extending to and just beyond three aligned 18th-century upright gravestones, which may be conjectured to be at or near where the high altar stood within the church (p. 82). Perhaps, in time, it may be possible permanently to expose the foundational remains of the church and abbey buildings, for the sake of better informing interested visitors, and providing visible and tangible evidence of this religious and historic Christian site.

Some further enlightenment on the layout of Soulseat Abbey has resulted from an archaeological survey carried out there in 1991 by members of the Archaeology Projects Glasgow, a unit of the University of Glasgow, at the request of Dumfries & Galloway Regional Council and Historic Scotland. Two sites were surveyed, using electronic and trenching methods: one site in the field in the mid-northern area of the promontory, the other site in the mid-southern area of the promontory, within and at the northern end of the walled garden (p. 83). At neither site were foundational remains discovered. Commenting on the garden area survey, the report (APG 42-1991) states:

> It would appear that the area enclosed by the walls of the garden has been used as a garden for many centuries. It is suggested that any remains of Soulseat Abbey would be situated further to the north of the promontory.

These surveys give support to the contention of the abbey-church location being east of the old manse building, and south of the field site surveyed and north of the walled garden area also surveyed.

In the 1908 edition of the Ordnance Survey map (25.3 inches to the mile) the central northern part of the promontory is shown as an orchard, fitting in with the findings of the 1991 survey.

The abbey title of *Sedes Animarum*, Soulseat, is found in both royal and papal medieval documents. Although Soulseat was its title, the abbey was in fact dedicated to St John the Evangelist. This is testified to in the official Premonstratensian publication *Monasticon Praemonstratense* Vol 2, by P Norberto Backmund (1952) and by Scott (Y, II, 336).

The title, Soulseat, seems to have been given to the abbey at the time of its Premonstratensian inception, if not just before that by the monks, Cistercian or otherwise, who may have been installed there by St Malachy. The latter's friend, St Bernard of Clairvaux, in his *Life of St Malachy* refers to the abbey loch as *viride stagnum*, the green pool. McKerlie (1877), too, says that in 1531, when David Vaux was Abbot of Soulseat, the monastery was called 'Greenloch, alias Saulseat', this being so from the green scum that floated on the surface at certain periods. This 'greening' of Soulseat Loch has evidently persisted over the centuries. It still occurs each year, about July or so, and remains while the weather is warm enough to sustain the green algae responsible for colouring the water. Public notices are displayed warning that the blue-green algal scum which gathers at the loch side may be harmful, both to humans and to animals, and to avoid contact with the scum and the water close to it. Despite this, fish abound in the loch and cattle graze on adjoining land. Soulseat is not lacking in charm and loveliness.

Abbots of Soulseat Abbey

	From	To
Christianus		
Michael		
Johannes	1273	
Nicolaus Gordon?		1334?
Finlay	1393	
Patrick McChaquhirky (Makehquhirty)		1458
Gilbert McWilnane	1458	
Gilbert Kennedy	*c.* 1470	
	c. 1460	
Quintinus (Quentin) Vaus	1493	*c.* 1529
David Vaus (coadjutor)	1525	
(abbot)	1529	1532
James Johnston	1532	1545
	*1533	*1546
John Johnston	1545	1600
	*1546	*1598

Michael is recorded as the first Premonstratensian Abbot of Soulseat (B, 102). Christianus may have preceded him as abbot of an earlier Cistercian or Augustinian foundation at Soulseat. Perhaps there is some link between the Christianus associated with Soulseat and Christianus who was the Bishop of Galloway from 1154 to 1186. Reid (K, 92) supports the contention that Christian is mistakenly listed abbot in the 12th century, and that he is probably being confused with Christian, bishop of Galloway, who died on 7 October, 1186.

With the exception of dates from other sources, particularly (K, 92-7), shown with asterisks, the above list is given in 'Monasticon Praemonstratense' id est Historia Circariarum atque Canoniarum Candidi et Canonici Ordinis Praemonstratensis. Auctore P. Norberto Backmund O. Praem. Ecclesiae Windbergensis in Bavaria Canonico. (Tomus Secundus) Straubing 1952. Cl. Attenkofersche Buchdruckerei.

Access: *OS Map Ref NX 1006 5869*

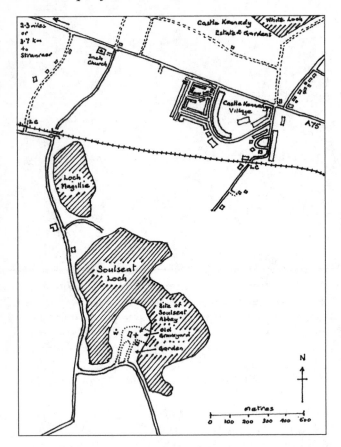

Turn south off the A75 road at Inch Parish Church, near the village of Castle Kennedy. The side road passes Loch Magillie and just beyond that is Soulseat Loch. Half a kilometre along the lochside road, turn left for the entrance to Meadowsweet Herb Garden and the site of Soulseat Abbey. The property is private and has public opening times in season.

Clayshant Parish Church

This is a sad story.

Clayshant is probably the next oldest church site in the Rhins, after Kirkmadrine. It is said to be contemporary with Kirkmadrine. It may date from the 5th century, but its foundation may have been as late as the 8th century. It is situated in an area of sand (and gravel) dunes, between Sandhead and Dunragit, beside Luce Bay.

Clayshant, as it is known today, has variously been called Clayshank and Clachshant. The latter is from the Gaelic *clach seanta*, translated as 'The Holy Stone'. Just why the church on this site should have this title is lost in antiquity. It may be conjectured that the title is derived from a custom which seems to have prevailed in the 8th-century Northumbrian period. Many places originally did not have built churches but 'field churches'. The latter consisted of a consecrated burial ground and a stone or wooden cross, which served as a meeting point for prayer. A shrine, with relics of a saint, may also have been placed in such a site to invoke protection for the burial ground and local congregation. In those years such field churches would be visited from time to time by bishop or priest for the sake of baptisms, burials and Mass. So, it may be that the early stone cross, marking this site as a field church, gave rise to its name 'The Holy Stone'.

By the medieval period a stone-built church was on this site and this Catholic parish church building survived here until well after the 16th-century Reformation, at which time it came under the authority of the new national reformed Church in Scotland.

In 1427, Alexander Vaus, bishop of Whithorn, appropriated this parish church of 'Clachshank' to the capitular mensa of Whithorn (K, 16). It was on 9 August 1427 that Pope Martin V gave the mandate to the Provost of Lincluden to confirm the appropriation if he deemed it fit (Cal. Papal Regs., Letters, vii, 526). Thus the church became a vicarage under the jurisdiction of the Premonstratensian Priory of Whithorn, and so continued until after the Reformation (N, 149). But on 3 December 1541 the patronage of the vicarage was exercised by the crown during the vacancy of the see. The late holder on this occasion was a canon of Whithorn (ibid, 149).

Robert Watson, a secular priest, was vicar of Clayshant parish on

26 February 1557 (z, 41). Dr Gordon Donaldson (0, 43), writing about Catholic priests who were vicars of Galloway parishes at the time of the Reformation states that while there were explanations why some of these joined the reformers and others did not, 'there was, indeed, only one vicar who clearly did not serve in the reformed church and for whom neither explanation nor excuse can be offered — Robert Watson (Clayshant)'. He seems to have continued in that post through the early Reformation period.

John Gibson, possibly friar of Wigtown, was minister at Clayshant in 1563. A person named Thomson is recorded as reader that same year. A Deed, dated 3 May 1568 (Reg. of Deeds, ix, 388) records Robert Watson as still the vicar of Clayshant. He died in or before 1581 (ibid, 60). From 1568 to 1572, John Gibson is recorded as exhorter at Clayshant and as minister there in 1574. (He also had oversight of Kirkmaiden church in 1574). During this time, too, James Law is recorded as reader in Clayshant parish in 1571-72 and in 1574 (z, 41). In 1576 Michael Hawthorn seems to have had responsibility for Clayshant parish as part of a multiple charge, which included Toskerton, Kirkmaiden, Leswalt and Kirkcolm. Sometime between 1576 and 1580, he resided at Clayshant, and then moved from there to Kirkcolm, where, while still retaining his multiple charge, he died, seemingly, in 1585 (x, 759 & 773).

Before 20 June 1618, Clayshant was united with the parish of Stoneykirk, as also was the parish of Kirkmadrine (Toskerton) (ibid, 773). It would seem that from that time onwards the church at Clayshant was allowed to deteriorate.

Timothy Pont carried out surveying work in Galloway in *c.* 1595. His records were used in the production of Johan Blaeu's map of Galloway in 1654. Klachshant is shown as an extant building.

Robert Morden does not include Clayshant in his undetailed map of Scotland in 1687.

Whether or not the church was still in use, Clayshant is indicated in General William Roy's map of the Rhins area in *c.* 1747.

In the Imperial Gazetteer of Scotland, in 1854, it is recorded: 'Vestiges of Clachshant church may still be seen on the farm of Clayshank.' (R, 758)

In 1877, McKerlie (H, II, 157) writes that Clachshant, or the Holy Stone, is situated on Clayshant Farm, but states that nothing now remains but a moss-covered stone here and there to mark the spot.

It would seem from this evidence that the actual church building

Excavated site of Clayshant Parish Church, with Culmore Farm in the right-hand background.

at Clayshant fell into disrepair between the 17th and 18th centuries, and was certainly ruinous and largely obscure by the mid 19th century.

The loss by desuetude and dereliction is a tragedy, especially when what is lost is irreplaceable and of such importance from a heritage point of view. But what was to follow makes one weep.

Some of the elderly family members who lived at Clayshant Farm from the 1930s to the 1960s do not recollect any discernible remains at the site of the church, or, in one case, said that there were some steps, but nothing else. The property passed into other hands, and since the 1970s has been extensively and systematically excavated for sand and gravel and stones.

Today, on the very site of the old Clayshant church there is a huge excavated area, from 5 to 6 metres deep. Not only was this very ancient Christian historical site devastated and any foundational remains scooped up and removed, but graves were disinterred. The burial ground around the church would have been used as such for some 16 centuries. Its hallowed or historical importance was obviously not recognised.

This is reminiscent of the passage in Scripture, where the prophet Jeremiah expresses God's lament:

Many shepherds have laid my vineyard waste,
have trampled down my inheritance
to a deserted wilderness.
They have made it a mournful, desolate place,
desolate before me.
The whole land is devastated
and no one takes it to heart.
— Jeremiah 12:10-11

In a report made by The Royal Commission on the Ancient Historical Monuments of Scotland, No. 26 (1987) it states:

> There are no visible remains of the medieval parish church of Clayshant, which evidently stood on a slight eminence 450 metres ENE of Culmore steading. The area of the burial-ground is now being quarried for gravel, and skeletal remains are visible in one of the quarry sections.

This official site visit was made in April, 1986.

What a sorry, sad and tragic loss this is. I almost weep as I write, at the thought. Such sites are to be treasured for what they are. Even now, out of respect, the site should not be allowed to be forgotten.

Access: *OS Map Ref NX 1077 5225*

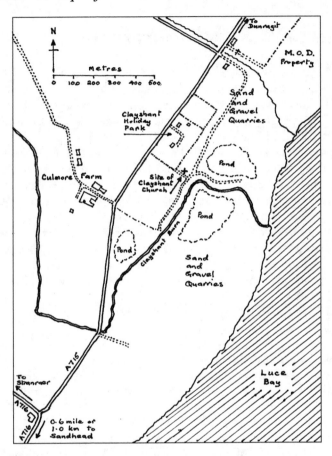

At present the site is on private property, though accessible with permission. It is most easily reached through the caravan park which is in operation at present on the east side of the A715 road between Dunragit and Sandhead, near Culmore Farm. The owners of the caravan park may allow you to park your car there and walk through to the site of the old Clayshant Church and former churchyard.

Inch Parish Church

There are two major lochs within Castle Kennedy estate: Black Loch, formerly known as Loch Crindil or Loch Inch Cryndil, to the north-east; and White Loch, formerly known as Loch of the Inch, to the south-west. On the mid-west side of White Loch there is a small island, known as the Inch, (sometimes, perhaps erroneously, referred to as Inch Crindil). There is a tradition that the earliest parish church of Inch stood on this island (D, 59). The title Inch is probably derived from the Gaelic *Innse*, for an islet or island. This derivation suggests that the earliest church here would be of Celtic origin, perhaps as early as the 8th century. But its actual date of origin is not recorded nor known. Its location on the island may have been for security reasons or it may suggest a little monastic establishment. By the early 19th century only the last traces of the burial ground associated with the original church could be roughly identified on Inch Island.

> 'The Manor Place of Inch' is said to have stood on the island in the White Loch 930 metres south-south-west of Lochinch Castle. In 1968, however, when the island was visited by the Officers of the Ordnance Survey, no visible remains were recorded. The manor is on record in 1433/4, 1482, and also in 1546, when the bishops were dispossessed of the property. Although it was probably abandoned early in the 17th century, on completion of nearby Castle Kennedy, there remained in 1684 'a little house' to which the Earl of Cassillis used to retire. (ibid, 63)

During the medieval period the Manor of Inch was a seat (or a residence) of the Bishop of Galloway (K, 87). As evidence of this, the Charter, dated 11 January 1433/4 by Alexander Vaus, Bishop of Whithorn, of the parish church of St Nicolas of Longcaster to the Priory of Whithorn, is shown as 'issued at the manor of Inche' (ibid, 22). Reid (ibid, 21) says that the bishop's residence at Innysmacrinyl was on the spit of land between the two lochs, Loch of Inch and the Black Loch. McKerlie (H, 1, 148) supports this contention. He remarks:

> [The Manor Place of Inch] is stated to have been built on an island — possibly near where Castle Kennedy stands; for, though not quite cut off from the land, it is all but surrounded with water.

It would seem that about the 11th century a medieval parish church was built, to replace the earlier Celtic one. This medieval church was not situated, like its predecessor, on Inch Island, but was nearby, on the mainland, on the west edge of the White Loch. The church stood within the surviving walled burial ground. This enclosure, in the Middle Ages, consisted of an earth-and-stone bank, up to 5 metres thick and 1.3 metres high. All that remains of the medieval parish church of Inch is the turf-covered outline of a robbed rectangular building measuring 18 metres by 9 metres. Adjacent to this and on its north-west side there are indications of a structure 7 metres square, which might possibly be a later burial-enclosure. In addition, in the south-east part of the main burial ground there are the turf-covered remains of a rectangular building measuring 9 metres by 5 metres. (D, 59)

Within this main burial ground, in 1936, a cross-incised stone slab was discovered. It measured 0.86 metres long, 0.16 metres wide, and 0.05 metres thick. It was engraved with the outline of a Latin Cross with an open median-incised shaft, wedge-shaped arms, transomed head and central boss (ibid, 59).

There are quite a number of remaining gravestones in the central area of the churchyard. About a quarter of them date from the 18th century and the remainder largely from the 19th century. Some are weather-worn and the inscriptions indiscernible. Nearly all of these gravestones face eastwards.

An enduring memory is that of visiting this medieval site by the lochside on a sunny February morning and walking through the peacefulness of the churchyard, which was then carpetted with snowdrops.

Historical records (Cassillis Charters, No. 653), (N, 150), show that the medieval parish church of Inch had been annexed to the bishopric of Galloway by the reign of John Baliol (1293-1297). Both parsonage and vicarage continued to be so annexed up until the time of the Reformation in 1560, the cure being served by a vicar pensioner (A, 84).

In the Register of John le Romayne (ii, 84n, 125), a church in the Rhins of Galloway, that of St Mary and St Michael, which has not been identified, is recorded as being annexed to the bishopric of Galloway in 1277. Cowan (A, 171) says that this 'is possibly to be equated with the church of Inch which is found so appropriated in the reign of John Baliol'.

In 1450, Inch Parish Church continued to come under the diocesan jurisdiction of the Bishop of Galloway, who sometimes resided locally at the Manor Place of Inch. Diocesan property at Inch bordered on that of Glenluce Abbey to the east. Just over two kilometres eastwards from the medieval Inch Church there was Balnab Farm. It was situated in land belonging to Inch, but the Abbot of Glenluce claimed that he had inherited rights over this property. In consequence, there was a dispute between the Bishop of Galloway and the Abbot of Glenluce as to which of them should receive tiends from the farm. According to Scott (Y, II, 336), Balnab, named from the Gaelic *Baile an Aib*, meaning 'the Abbot's place', was a possession of the abbots of Glenluce. This dispute was mutually presented for resolution on 10 September 1450; the charter of agreement survives and is signed by Henry, bishop of Galloway and Galter abbot of Glenluce (K, 69).

John McCrekane, vicar of Inch, witnessed two charters dated 2 March 1505/6, and 11 November 1506 (ibid, 187).

From perhaps as early as the 8th century, and in a more accessible way from about the 11th century, until the middle of the 16th century, a Catholic church at Inch had been catering to the spiritual needs of the local people.

On 25 March, 1516, a charter by David Arnot, bishop of Galloway, constituted Gilbert, earl of Cassillis, Lord Kennedy, as bailie of all the lands of the bishopric of Galloway within the sheriffdom of Wigtown, and also captain, constable and keeper of the manor place and loch of Inch lying within the Rynnis of Galloway (ibid, 26).

At the period of the Reformation, the parish church of Inch had two chapels within its jurisdiction (Y, II, 336): St John's Chapel in Stranraer and St Patrick's Chapel in Portpatrick. Symson (G, 57) also records 'the parish of Portpatrick, which was once belonging to, and was a part of the parish of Inch, and to this day is yet called the black quarter thereof.'

It is recorded that William McDowell, who was an ordained secular priest from at least 1547/8, held the vicarage pensionary of Inch in 1559 and was in possession of both Inch and Leswalt from 1561-72. The secular priest, Cuthbert Adair, who was chaplain at Whithorn in 1550, was exhorter at Inch in 1563 and in 1567-68. Thomas Alexander was reader in 1570-74. Mr James Fothringhame, minister of Glenluce, had oversight of Inch Church in 1574 (O, 56 & Z, 108).

After the Reformation in 1560, the medieval Inch church building was taken over by the Reformed Church, and it continued to be used thus as the parish church until it was replaced, probably in the 17th century, by the church building that now stands roofless in the north-west corner of the burial ground. This church building was extensively remodelled in the late 18th century, and was abandoned about 1862 on completion of the present Inch Parish Church of Scotland, which is located one kilometre to the south, immediately on the other side of the main A75 road.

The Pont-Blaeu map of 1654, for which Timothy Pont surveyed Galloway *c*. 1595, records the church at Loch of the Inch on the west mainland near Inch Island. This would probably be the medieval church dating from about the 11th century.

Nearby, on the east side of the White Loch, are the remains of the medieval Castle Kennedy:

> This stronghold of the Kennedys was built by the fifth Earl of Cassillis in 1607, and must have supplanted an older keep, of which it is recorded that John, Lord Kennedy, was appointed keeper in 1482. In the latter half of the 17th century it passed with the adjoining lands to Sir John Dalrymple (afterwards Viscount Stair) and his descendants. The castle was accidentally destroyed by fire in 1716, and was not restored. (E, 18).

The ruins of Castle Kennedy, its gardens and its parkland, are open to the public, in season.

Between the north end of the White Loch and the west side of the Black Loch stands Lochinch Castle. It was completed between 1864 and 1867, and is the private residence of the Earl of Stair.

> The old village of Inch is depicted on 18th and 19th century maps to the west of the burial ground on the west side of White Loch, where the medieval church and its replacement stood. This village was probably removed in the 1860s when the policies of Lochinch Castle were remodelled. All that is now visible to the south-west of the burial ground is a possible platform (9 metres by 5 metres) and a few low scarps. (D, 70).

The nearby Castle Kennedy village was developed, replacing old Inch village.

Access: *OS Map Ref NX 1025 6087*

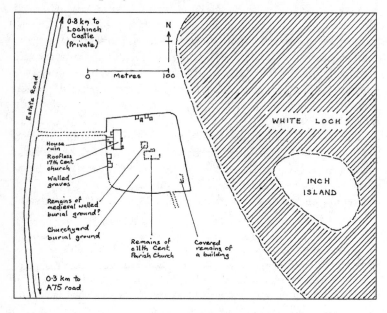

The site of the *c.* 11th- and *c.* 17th-century churches is reached via the private road leading to Lochinch Castle. Entry to this road is from the A75, just opposite the present-day Inch Parish Church. About a kilometre along the estate private road, on the right-hand side, there is the old cemetery enclosure containing the site and remains of the two earlier period churches. Although not accessible, the nearby Inch Island, where tradition says the first of the four successive Inch churches stood, can be viewed from the mainland cemetery enclosure.

Stoneykirk Parish Church

The village of Stoneykirk is named after the church. The first church here was built probably between the 12th and 14th centuries. There are no records of its exact date of origin. The church was dedicated to St Stephen. Stephen's Kirk seems to have been locally expressed as Steeniekirk, then Stainiekirk, and finally Stoneykirk. Thus we have the saint's name changed linguistically in time to express the means by which he was martyred. St Stephen is proto-martyr of the Church; his death by stoning is recounted in the Acts of the Apostles.

Up to the period of the Reformation in the 16th century, St Stephen's Church lived in the shadow of the proto-church of the whole Rhins area, Kirkmadrine Church, which was some 5 kilometres south of Stoneykirk. In 1547, the lay patronage of the church in Stoneykirk was in dispute between the McDowells of Freugh and the McDowells of Garthland (M, V, 438).

Neil McDowell, a diocesan priest in Galloway, was parson at Stoneykirk on 4 March 1552 (z, 226). His name appears in a register dated 1554 (o, 56). He is mentioned again as parson at Stoneykirk on

26 March 1557 (z, 226). After the Reformation he attested a charter dated 22 July 1561, in which he is described as 'parson of Steinkirk' (K, 81). In 1562-3, he is recorded as reader and allowed the third of the parsonage and vicarage of Stoneykirk (z, 226).

John Gibson, possibly friar of Wigtown, was minister here in 1563. Donald McCulloch was possibly reader in 1565. John Gibson again is noted as exhorter in 1567-72, and was minister in 1574 (ibid, 226).

At the time of the Reformation in 1560, St Stephen's Church was a parish church under the jurisdiction of the Diocese of Galloway: it was a free parsonage and not appropriated, like most other parish churches, to a monastery or religious order. Within a period of sixty years after the Reformation, Stoneykirk became the centre of parish life in the area, and on or before 1618 the parish of St Stephen's, Stoneykirk, had subsumed the ancient parishes of Kirkmadrine and Clayshant (x, 773). Catholicism was replaced by Act of Parliament in 1560, and from that time Presbyterian Church life took over. This was the case at St Stephen's Church, which continued in such use up to the early part of the 19th century. It was in 1827 that a new church was built on the same site to replace the original medieval one. Nothing remains of the medieval church. On the site now stands the unused 1827 church, which, being quite commodious, has been overtaken by changing social and ecclesiastical circumstances and has been out of use since the beginning of 1988. It stands within the confines of the original churchyard as a sentinel or memorial of the centuries, people, priests and ministers, and all that is gathered together in the life of St Stephen's Parish, stretching from the medieval period to the 20th century. It has played its part and takes its place in the Christian heritage of the Rhins.

It is interesting to note that at the north-western end of Stoneykirk parish, about 4.5 km from Portpatrick, there are two farms, North or Little Spittal and South or Meikle Spittal. A mill, the stream and the nearby bay are named after some spittal that was in the area in the Middle Ages. Such spittals were the early forerunners of what became hospitals. Lynch (P2, 211) writes:

> In the 12th century, the hospital became a common feature in the urban landscape. The medieval hospital was called in contemporary language 'God's House' [*Domus dei*, or *Maison-dieu* in French].

Such spittals were located widely and provided primitive and basic care for the sick, and especially hospitality for those on journeys. Such provision seemingly featured in this part of the Rhins. It would seem that such an institution here coincided with the medieval erection of St Stephen's Church at Stoneykirk. MacQueen (Q2, 29) writes:

> Almost equidistant [2 or 3 miles] from Killantringan Bay, Portpatrick and Port of Spittal, three of the best landing places on the west coast, stands the modern Spittal [spiteal] 'a place of hospitality',

which he considers to have been a place of accommodation for pilgrims to Whithorn in the period from the 12th to the 16th century.

Access: *OS Map Ref NX 0891 5322*

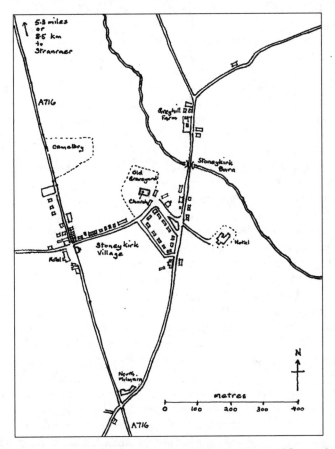

The churchyard is located in the centre of the village of Stoneykirk, about 7 kilometres south-south-east of Stranraer.

Chapel of St John, Stranraer

Up until the 15th and 16th centuries, Stranraer does not appear to have been very prominent in the Rhins area. The fact is that it was not one place but two. At that time the stream running north into Loch Ryan acted as a boundary, to the west of which lay the village or small town of Stranraer, and to the east of which lay the village or small town of Chapel. The Johan Blaeu map of 1654, for which Timothy Pont surveyed Galloway *c.* 1595, includes these two places, indicating nothing noteworthy at Stranraer, but prominently depicting a church in that part known as Chapel. In the Blaeu map, Stranraer is printed as Stronrawyr.

Various explanations are given for the derivation of the name Stranraer. It could be from the Gaelic *Stron* and *reanhar*, meaning the thick or clumsy nose. An alternative Gaelic derivation would be from *Strath-an-radhair*, or *Strath-an-rogha-fhevir*, meaning the valley of good grass or pasture. A Norse derivation is possible from *Strond* and *Strendir*, for coastland, strand or shore. Pont refers to it as *Stronrawyr*. It is also referred to in a 14th-century charter (H, I, 130) as *Stranrever*. A further derivation is from the early English *Strand-raw*, meaning row of houses on the strand. In 1596 the village was erected a burgh of barony, under Adair of Kilhilt, by a charter in which the name is written as Stranrawer (ibid, 132). Variations of its name, such as Stronerawer, Stronavir, Stranraiver and Stranraer, are still evident in charters of the 16th and 17th centuries.

It was in 1617 that Stranraer became a royal burgh.

Although with the passage of time, Stranraer was to emerge as the victor and Chapel as the vanquished, it seems that up until about the end of the 16th century Chapel enjoyed more prominence than its adjoining neighbour Stranraer. McKerlie (ibid, 132) goes so far as to say:

> At one time Stranraer was called Chappell, from the chapel of St John, which then alone marked the spot. This chapel, Sir A Agnew informs us, was founded by one of the three sisters of Bishop Adair.

It was built in the 15th century (c, 34). About 1511, the Adairs built a castle close to St John's Chapel. It was around this 16th-century tower-house or castle that the town of Stranraer developed. Kennedy of Ochtrelure got possession of the castle. In 1567 Hew Kennedy settled near St John's Chapel and was styled Kennedy of Chappell. By 1623 John Kennedy was in possession of Chappell, and in 1635 he is styled as of Stranrawer. This fits in with Stranraer becoming a royal burgh in 1617, and subsuming what had hitherto been the independent Chapel.

Although united in one burgh, the continued use of the two place names is witnessed by Symson (G, 60), who, in 1684, writes:

> Stranrawer, called also the Chapel. This is a Burgh Royal lately enroll'd…On the east end of the town, there is a good house pertaining to Sir John Dalrymple, younger of Stair, call'd the Castle of the Chapel, where also there is a chapel now ruinous, from whence all on the east side of the bourn is called the Chapel. Betwixt this house and the kirk, there runns a bourn or strand, so that perhaps the town should be spell'd Strandrawer. This house and the crofts about it, though I have diligently enquir'd thereanent, yet I could never certainly learn to which parish it really pertaines; some asserting that it belongs to the parish of Inch; others, that it belongs to the parish of Stranrawer, though not lyable to the jurisdiction of the burgh there, as some alledge.

The pre-Reformation Chapel of St John was never a parish church. As a chapel it came within the jurisdiction of the parish of Inch. St John's Chapel would cease to be Catholic from 1560, the time of the Reformation. Little is known of its use from that time until the first Presbyterian Parish Church was built in Stranraer in 1766. It is reported that St John's Chapel was pulled down in the late 17th or 18th century (c, 34). Nothing now remains of the chapel. Even its dedication is clouded, since it could be dedicated to St John, the apostle and evangelist, or to St John the Baptist. It was more probably the former.

The castle passed from the possession of the Kennedys to the Dalrymples of Stair. It was used as a jail over the centuries. In the early part of the 20th century it was being used as a merchant's store. It is now a museum.

From inconspicuous beginnings Stranraer has become the largest, busiest and most populated centre in the Rhins. Its Christian antecedents are continued in the various denominational churches in the town. Among these churches is St Joseph's, which is the only Catholic Church in the entire Rhins area.

Access: *OS Map Ref NX 0607 6080*

The site of the pre-Reformation Chapel of St John is not now known with certainty, but it is known to have been in the vicinity of the castle, which still stands in the centre of Stranraer.

Chapel Patrick, Portpatrick

Throughout the early Celtic period of the Church in Scotland, from the 5th century to the 11th century, there would be much to-ing and fro-ing between Scotland and Ireland. Various little ports were used for coracles and later for fishing and sailing boats. Portpatrick, first with its natural harbour, and much later with its constructed harbour, increasingly, up until the late 19th century, developed as a ferry port for trade and traffic between Scotland and Ireland. From the 5th century onwards, religious and clerical passengers would be included among the seafaring travellers.

In time, a chapel was built in the little harbour village of Portpatrick. This little Chapel Patrick would probably have accommodation for the visiting regular or secular priest and further accommodation for clerical or lay travellers. The exact date of the erection of Chapel Patrick is not known; it is likely to have been built between about the 7th to the 11th centuries. It continued in Catholic use right up to the Reformation in 1560, when it was taken over for Scottish Reformed Church use. It seemingly continued to be used as such up until the 1620s. Up until then Chapel Patrick and the general area of Portpatrick came under the Parish of Inch, and the area was known as the Black Quarter of Inch.

In the period just before 1620 Portpatrick was known as Portree. In 1620 Viscount Montgomery acquired the Barony of Portree, and changed the name of the village to Port Montgomery. After a few years the property changed hands again and it was renamed Dunskey by the Revd James Blair. But it came eventually to be called Portpatrick.

In 1628 a charter granted by Charles I detached the lands of Portree (Portpatrick) and Kilhilt and Sorbie (near Wigtown) and formed them into a separate parish. It was also ordained that the decayed little church at Portpatrick, which was in the process of being rebuilt, should become the parish church. In 1630, another charter suppressed Soulseat Abbey and granted as an endowment to the new Portpatrick parish the unappropriated revenues, which had belonged to the Abbey, of both the parish churches of Soulseat and Kirkmaiden.

Thus a new parish church, dedicated to St Andrew, was constructed between 1622 and 1629. It was of cruciform structure, with a round tower at its west end. The tower, which is four storeys in height, with several small windows on each floor, may have been purposely built as a watch tower. Even today one can see the date 1629 inscribed on one of the ruined gables at the east end of the church. This St Andrew's Kirk ceased to be used in 1842 and is presently maintained in its ruined state. It is said to have been built upon the site of the original Celtic Chapel Patrick. it may be that part of the old Chapel Patrick was incorporated into the construction of the 1629 replacement Kirk of St Andrew. In this case it is likely that the earlier chapel, being rectangular in shape, would therefore make up the east-west axis of the replacement 1629 cruciform-shaped kirk. It is suggested that the surviving tower may be an integral part of the original Chapel Patrick (E, 137). It is built of soft, red sandstone, much decayed by weathering, while the 1629 church is built of a grey-coloured hardstone, which has weathered well.

The churchyard, within the confines of an old stone wall, contains many graves. The graveyard may go back as far as fourteen or fifteen centuries.

Access: *OS Map Ref NW 9998 5421*

The ruins of the 17th-century Kirk of St Andrew, on the probable site of the earlier Chapel Patrick, are off Patrick Street, in the centre of Portpatrick. There is limited car parking nearby, but plentiful parking facilities around the harbour. The ruins are always open to the public.

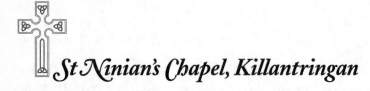

St Ninian's Chapel, Killantringan

Killantringan at various times has been called Killanringan, Killantringan, Kilringan, Kiltringan, Killentringzen and Killamtrinzeane. The name is said to be derived from the Gaelic *cill sheant Ringain* (the Gaelic sh is silent), which translates as the Chapel of St Ringan. *Ringan* is the Gaelic form of Ninian. MacQueen (Q2, 19) argues that since the Gaelic form of Killantringan contains the prefixed title *sheant* or saint, the name in this form cannot be earlier than the 12th century.

No records exist of the erection date or actual site of the chapel dedicated to St Ninian at this coastal spot, a little more than three kilometres north of Portpatrick. Though it may have been built earlier, perhaps 7th to 11th century, MacQueen (ibid, 28, 29) puts the date as the 12th or 13th century and suggests that the chapel was built for the use of pilgrims on their way to Whithorn, Killantringan Bay providing a good landing place for those crossing by sea from Ireland.

It is included in the Pont-Blaeu map of 1654 as Killitrinzen. No other later maps include the name until the Ordnance Maps of the 19th and 20th centuries.

Scott (Y, 11, 350) states there was a Chapel of St Ninian at Kilantringen.

There are no remains of the St Ninian Chapel at Killantringan, nor any sign of a burial ground.

Two features of the area retain a link through their names: one is Killantringan Farm, the other is Killantringan Bay.

Access: *OS Map Ref NW c981 564*

On foot, over 3 kilometres along the Southern Upland Way footpath northwards from Portpatrick.

By car, approaching Portpatrick on the A77 road, turn northwards for some 3 kilometres along the A764 road, then turn left (westward) on to the minor, surfaced road, leading to Killantringan. Near to and above the bay there is parking space. The lighthouse is nearby.

St Catherine's Chapel, Eldrickhill

In this field in front of Eldrickhill Farm, there are two adjacent wells, the older of which is nearer to the farm buildings and is known as St Catherine's Well. A medieval chapel, dedicated to St Catherine, stood in this vicinity.

Ainslie's map of 1782 shows Eldrickhill lying on one of the routes used between Portpatrick and Stoneykirk and the eastern parts of Galloway and beyond. As such, St Catherine's Chapel on this site would have been a wayside-chapel or a chapel-of-ease, one associated too with a burial ground.

The dedication to St Catherine poses the question — which St Catherine? It would seem to be either St Catherine of Alexandria or St Catherine of Siena.

There is a tradition, without much certainty, of the life of St Catherine of Alexandria; even the period of her life is unknown, but it would seem she lived in Alexandria during the era of the Roman Empire. There is a traditional belief that because of her profession of Christian Faith, she was put to death on a spiked wheel (whence our 'catherine-wheel'). As a Christian martyr, she was venerated in Eastern Christendom, but from the time of the Crusades, from 1095 to 1396, her popularity was even greater in the West, continuing at a peak until the 18th century. Numerous churches were dedicated in her honour and her feastday, 25 November, was kept with great solemnity. She was venerated as the patroness of maidens and women sudents, of philosophers, preachers and apologists, of wheelwrights, millers and others.

St Catherine of Siena (1347-1380) was a spiritually infuential figure of her time. She was instrumental in ending the seventy-four-year exile of the popes at Avignon in France. She engaged in many charitable works, drew admiration, won over people to good and, in general, was recognised for the holiness of her life. The Church canonised her a saint in 1461.

If the chapel at Eldrickhill was dedicated to St Catherine of Alexandria, it could date from as early as the 12th century. If it was dedicated to St Catherine of Siena, then it would be more likely to date from the 14th century. Irrespective of whichever of these two saints the Eldrickhill chapel is dedicated to, it would seem that this chapel was founded later than most of the other chapels and churches in the Rhins. It may be the case that it was built as a chapel-of-ease for the emergent medieval St Stephen's parish church, at Stoneykirk, which is reckoned to have been built probably between the 12th and 14th centuries.

Another possible influential factor could be the establishment, in the 13th century, of a fortified house in the neighbourhood, affording more protection for the area and perhaps providing patronage. McKerlie (H, I, 52), writing in 1877, states:

A square tower which stood on the lands of Garthland (2.0 kilometres from Eldrickhill) until a few years ago bore the date 1274 on the battlements. This is believed to have been the tower of the strong old house occupied by the family [McDowall] in former times, and the date carries it back to the era of Robert the Bruce.

Again, in 1877, McKerlie (H, II, 164) comments that

(this church at Eldrickhill) was situated on the north-western boundary of Stoneykirk parish, at the village of Eldrig Hill; but not a stone now remains,and the site can alone be traced by the well, dedicated to St Catherine, which is still used. A burial ground is supposed to have surrounded the church.

There is some evidence that this chapel was, indeed, associated also with a burial ground.

During the first half of the 19th century, workmen, digging in a small enclosure nearby, unearthed features 'resembling old graves in which was found some pieces of decayed wood which was quite black as at some past time burned' (c, 26).

The Historical Monuments (Scotland) Commission Report on Wigtownshire, in 1912, says: 'It is stated that a graveyard formerly lay around or near the well' (E, 158).

At this site today there remains a well, St Catherine's Well (map ref NX 0612 5442), not far from the present farm of Eldrickhill. The well is now covered with a large, horizontal-laid stone slab, measuring about 1.8 metres by 0.5 metre. 'The Chapel dedicated to St Catherine is said to have stood in the vicinity of the well, some 80 metres north-east of Eldrickhill farmhouse' (C, 26).

The present farm name of Eldrickhill has, in the past, been written as Eldrig Hill (OS Map 1908). McKerlie (H, II, 151 & 175) says that the derivation of Eldrick, Elrig or Eldrig is from the Norse *Al* (in Anglo-Saxon *Eeal*) meaning all, and the Norse *Hryggr* (in English *Rigg*) meaning a ridge.

Half a kilometre north-westwards from Eldrickhill the road reaches the upper slope of Bean Hill. From the road, at this spot, there is a fine panoramic view looking northwards to Loch Ryan and south-eastwards to Luce Bay.

Access: St Catherine's Well   *OS Map Ref NX 0612 5442*
        Chapel and burial ground *OS Map Ref NX c061 544*

Eldrickhill can be reached from the A77 Portpatrick road, by going south through Colfin Farm.

Kildonan Chapel, near Stoneykirk

Just off the B7042 road, between Sandhead and Portpatrick, there is the farm and associated cottages of Kildonan. At a radius of about 0.8 kilometre to the south and west skirts the Kildonnan Burn. In this vicinity a chapel dedicated to St Donnan of Eigg is said to have stood (Y, II, 353), (C, 27). Though this is presently a lesser route site, it is shown on Ainslie's map of 1782 as then on a road route leading from Portpatrick, through Mickle (South) Spittal, Kildonan, Stoneykirk and on to Glenluce. This ancient through route for travellers, from and to Portpatrick, would provide one reason for the existence of a chapel here. It may have been a wayside chapel, or a chapel-of-ease, or one associated with a local burial ground. It is likely to have been erected between the 7th and the 12th centuries.

Another explanation for the existence of this chapel is that a castle is said to have stood near Kildonan farmhouse (C, 33). McKerlie, in 1877, writes:

> Between Kildonan and Bog End farm houses there was a fort; but the site is now under tillage, we regret to say. What can be made of it gives the appearance of a square. Whether it was Roman or Danish cannot be ascertained, but the latter is believed.

There are now no visible remains of this castle. The chapel in this area may have been provided by the castle incumbent. On the Pont-Blaeu map of 1654, Kildonnen is shown with the figure of what appears to be a church or a castle. McKerlie (H, II, 159), in 1877, writes: 'At Kildonan (Parish of Stoneykirk) no remains of a religious building are to be found, but that a chapel did stand there is to be believed.'

It is interesting that St Donnan is again commemorated with this third chapel in the Rhins area, the other two being Chapel Donnan, near Barsalloch to the north, and Kildonan Chapel, near Drummore to the south. This gives some indication of the esteem and veneration with which this martyr-saint was held in the hearts of the people. In the Rhins, at Kirkcolm, there was an ancient parish church dedicated to St Columba, who was St Donnan's abbot at Iona, before St Donnan was assignd to take a party of monks and found a new abbey on the Isle of Eigg. It was there, on Easter Day 618 that he and fifty-two monk companions were massacred by heathen raiders. Although St Columba is revered for his great spiritual leadership, holiness, and missionary endeavour, St Donnan, in giving his life, was also highly esteemed throughout Scotland and Ireland. Hence the reason for finding three chapels in the Rhins dedicated to St Donnan.

Access: **Chapel:** *OS Map Ref NX c05 51*
        Castle: *OS Map Ref NX c059 519*

Kildonan is about 3.0 kilometres south-west of Stoneykirk. It can be approached from Stoneykirk or Sandhead, or by the road westwards from Mains of Caldons Farm.

North Rhins

Kirkcolm Parish Church

Leswalt Parish Church

St Mary's Chapel, Kilmorie

Killiecuddican

Chapel Donnan, Balsarroch

St Bride's Chapel, East Kirkbryde

Topmalloch

Cairnhapple

Kirkcolm Parish Church

Among the Christian heritage sites in the Rhins, here lies a little gem.

Kirkcolm is the name of the village on the east side of the north Rhins. (For a short period in the 17th century it was called Stewarton). The village of Kirkcolm takes its name from an ancient parish church dedicated to St Columba. All that remains of the church now are its outlined foundation ruins, with some lower south wall sections up to 0.8 metre high. The old church occupied a rectangular area, some 17.5 metres long and 7.5 metres broad, in the knolled centre of its original churchyard, which is situated in what has become Corsewall Estate. The churchyard burial-ground is enclosed by traces of what may be an earlier perimeter comprising double banks and a medial ditch on the north and north-east, which converge on the east to form a single bank 5.5 metres thick and 1.2 metres high. The churchyard contains many graves, two mausoleums and quite a number of memorial stones, most of which are of the 18th and 19th centuries. The ancient grassy churchyard contains some trees, is encompassed by an old stone wall, and is in the lovely setting of the huge surrounding trees of the estate. It is a place of peace and loveliness, especially on a sunny day. By the stream, near the entrance to the churchyard, there is an ancient well, known as St Columba's Well.

No exact date is known of the building of the old Catholic church here, dedicated to St Columba. Cowan (A, 119) says it was also known as Kyraem in Rhinns. The church may have been erected as early as the 7th century or as late as the 11th century.

It was granted to New (Sweetheart) Abbey, near Dumfries, by Devorgilla de Baliol, possibly at the time of the abbey's foundation in 1273. However, the patronage alone seems to have been involved, the church being granted to the uses of the abbey by Adam de Lanark, Bishop of Galloway (1363-1378), and confirmed to the Cistercian monks of Sweetheart Abbey by Archibald, Earl of Douglas, in 1401. (ibid, 119).

In 1296, Alexander de Puntunby, the parson, swore fealty to Edward I, and obtained a writ to the Sheriff of Wigton for delivery of his property — the lands belonging to the Church (H, II, 120).

There is a record of William de Parlington as rector of Kirkcolm receiving ordination to the priesthood from Bishop Halton on 7 April 1302, on letters dimissory from Thomas de Kirkcudbright, Bishop of Galloway (K, iii).

At this time, two parish priests of St Columba's Church at Kirkcolm were to be elevated to the bishopric of Galloway. Thomas, resident priest at Kirkcolm, was appointed Bishop of Galloway on 31 December 1359, by Pope Innocent VI, having already been consecrated at Avignon, where the Pope was in residence. Thomas died after 2 September 1362, probably in 1363 (N, 140). The second priest, Thomas de Butil, had been the parish priest of Kirkcolm before being appointed to the provostry and vicarage of Maybole, then the vicarage of Dundonald and the churches of Abernyte and Kinkell. He was archdeacon of Whithorn (from 1410 or earlier) and an auditor of the papal palace of causes when he was made Bishop of Galloway on 14 June 1414. He died before or during 1422 (ibid, 141).

Evidently, from the 14th century, Kirkcolm Church was made a perpetual vicarage, but Sweetheart Abbey to which it was annexed apparently also took part of these fruits in the 15th century, while in the 16th century both parsonage and vicarage appear to have been annexed and the cure served by a vicar pensioner (A, 119). So, although the church is recorded as being a free parsonage in the 13th century, from the 14th century onwards, until the Reformation in

1560, it was held by the Cistercian monks of New (Sweetheart) Abbey and served by a vicar.

James McCallan, a secular priest, was vicar pensionary at Kirkcolm Church on 9 May 1541. He died before 13 September 1569. John McCrekane, another secular priest, was curate in this parish on 11 May 1556, and is reported as deceased curate before 24 February 1587. Alexander Hunter was exhorter in 1563, 1568, 1571-72 and reader in 1567, 1569 and 1574. John Gibson (minister of Clayshant) had oversight of the church in 1574 (z, 145). Scott (x, 773) records that Michael Hawthorn, who was minister at Toskerton in 1576, assumed multiple charge that year of Toskerton, Kirkmadin(?) in Ryns, Leswalt and Kirkcolm, and adds that 'he continued in 1580, and removed to Killemorie or Kirkcolm.' The same authority, Scott, states specifically elsewhere (ibid, 759) that it was to Kirkcolm that Michael Hawthorn moved.

The church then continued to be used by the Presbyterian Church of Scotland up until *c.* 1720, when it was extensively repaired. It was at this time that the Kilmorie Stone was brought from its original site at St Mary's Croft on Wig Bay, and used as a lintel above the western main doorway of the restored church. The church continued in use for a further century until its dismantling in 1821. The Kilmorie Stone stood in the grounds of Corsewall Estate until 1988, from which time it has been placed in the churchyard of the local Ervie-Kirkcolm Parish Church. (Full details about the Kilmorie Stone are given in a following section dealing with St Mary's Chapel, Kilmorie.)

The old Kirkcolm Church stood in serviceable use for between seven and twelve centuries. Its remaining stones are memorials to this long Church tradition, straddling both the Catholic and Protestant past.

The church's dedication to the Celtic saint, Columba, may suggest its origin being nearer the 7th century than the 11th century.

St Columba, as he is generally called in Scotland and elsewhere, was born about the year 521 in County Donegal, Ireland, of royal lineage. His baptismal name was Colm, Colum or Columba. In later life he was commonly called Colmcille. He became a priest monk in his native land, before travelling as a missionary with twelve companions in a coracle to land at Iona in the Hebrides of Scotland in the year 563. He was then about forty-two years of age. He and his fellow monks built their famous monastery there and from this centre did their missionary work among the Picts of the north and the Scots of the south. He died in the year 597. Butler writes:

His influence lasted on, extended until it came to dominate the churches of Scotland, Ireland and Northumbria. For three-quarters of a century and more, Celtic Christians in those lands upheld Columban traditions in certain matters of order and ritual in opposition to those of Rome itself, and the rule Columba had drawn up for his monks was followed in many of the monasteries of western Europe until it was superseded by the milder ordinances of St Benedict. (J, II, 509)

Whether or not St Columba ever visited the Rhins area of Galloway is not known, but the dedication of this ancient church of Kirkcolm, the Church of Columba, is a testimony of his holiness and fame .

St Columba was of the Uf Neill of the North of Ireland. One of his kinsmen was Conall, king of Scottish Dalriada. This linkage with the family name Conall or Connell may be associated with the naming of the large loch west of Kirkcolm as Loch Connell.

In the north-west area of the Rhins, near Corsewall Point, there is a well at Portmullin, which bears the name St Columba's Well. Evidently there was a cross by the well, which gave rise to the name Corsewell, adapted in time to Corsewall. This is both the name of the lighthouse point near St Columba's Well and the name of the estate that was developed round the site of the ancient St Columba's Church at Kirkcolm.

Despite the names associated with St Columba in this area and the traditional acceptance of this ancient parish church being dedicated to that saint, Brooke (1994, p. 75) points out that the pronunciation of the parish name has apparently always been 'Kirk-Cum', and that a papal letter (Reg Vat 322, unpublished in Scottish Record Office) gives the patron saint as St Cummin or Cummene. This saint is also known as Cumine the White. He was of Irish descent, the seventh abbot of Iona, who wrote a life of St Columba, and died in the year 669.

Access to Church remains: *OS Map Ref NX 0306 6885*

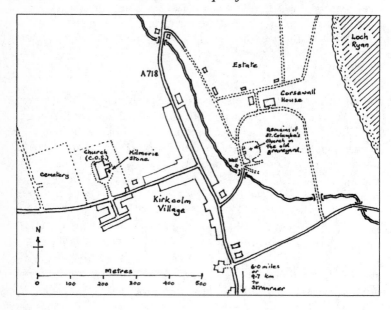

Cars may be parked in the village. It is a walk of only about 100 metres along the Corsewall Estate lane, until, to the right-hand side, there is the walled churchyard with its entrance gate. The churchyard is always open to visitors.

Leswalt Parish Church

The name 'Leswalt' is interesting. According to McKerlie (H,II,185):

> The name of the parish seems to be from the Anglo-Saxon word *Loesew*, a pasture, or *leswe*, in Irish, *leasur*, a meadow, the latter as given by Jamieson. Symson gives the pronunciation as Laswede. The word probably was taken from the Cymric *Aswellt*, pasture, land for grazing.

An alternative derivation is given by Sir Herbert Maxwell (1930, p. 195): he sees the name Leswalt derived from the Gaelic *Lios uillt*, genitive of *allt*, the fort of the glen, indicating the local Lochnaw Castle at the head of Aldouran Glen. There is doubt about that interpretation with the meaning of the Gaelic constituent words being: *allt, uillt* = stream, brook, and *lios, lise* = garden, orchard. A further interpretation is given by Sir Andrew Agnew (w, I, 123-4). The Greek word *ekklesia*, meaning assembly or church, was Latinised to *ecclesia*. Sir Andrew says:

> Eaglais is a Celtic adaptation of the Latin, appears in Terregles, originally Traveregles, the church lands (and in) Slewnagles (*s* omitted in Ordnance Survey), Leswalt, the church hill.

No early records exist that date the founding of this parish church. It is at least medieval, if not earlier. The two earliest documents referring to Leswalt Parish Church are recorded in Vatican Transcripts ii NO. 47, and Calendar of Entries in the Papal Registers — Petitions to the Pope, i, 595. They refer to the annexation of Leswalt Church to the custody of the Premonstratensian Canons of Tongland Abbey, near Kirkcudbright, by Michael MacKenlagh, who was the Bishop of Galloway from 1355 to 1359. The documents show the papal approval for this annexation was dated 25 May 1410 (K, 20). It is noted that for more than forty years before the papal approval the annexation had been initiated and implemented by Bishop Michael.

So it is not known if the origin of this parish church goes back to the Celtic or medieval period. Its origin lies somewhere probably between the 7th and 12th centuries.

Nearby is Lochnaw Castle. The original castle on an island in the loch was built probably during the 12th century. In 1426 the Agnews took over the property on acquiring the position of Constable of the area (ibid, 161-2). It was then that the present castle on the south shore of the loch replaced the earlier island one. Over the centuries the Agnews grew in prominence, becoming, from 1456, Hereditary Sheriffs of Wigtownshire. About 1663, the castle was altered and enlarged. No records exist of the links between local Lochnaw Castle and Leswalt Church in the pre-Reformation period. There were certainly links after the Reformation, and these are referred to later.

Locally, too, in the Middle Ages, the land around nearby Craigencross belonged to the Knights Templar. The name Craigencross, the Hill of the Cross, suggests that in the Templars' time there was a Cross at this site, symbolising Christ's redemption. The principal house of the Knights Templar in Scotland was at Temple, also known as Balantrodoch, in Midlothian.

In the 1120s, Hugh of Payen, a French knight in Palestine, sought to combine monastic life with military service. He and eight companions founded the first military religious order, the Knights of the Temple, so called because they were then based on the Temple Mount in Jerusalem. They undertook the monastic vows of poverty, chastity and obedience, but their innovation was to use their military skills to protect pilgrims in the Holy Land. About 1128, St Bernard of Clairvaux composed a written rule for the group, which was approved by Pope Honorius II. The Templars grew rapidly in numbers and wealth, especially through estates in Europe donated by admiring supporters of their work. They dressed in a white habit with a red cross and were headed by an official called the master. There were three constituent groups within the Templars: knights who fought, sergeants who aided them, and priest-chaplains who ministered to their spiritual needs.

Other contemporary military orders, including the Knights of the Hospital of St John, were instituted.

The Templars lost their original purpose with the fall of the Holy Land to the Muslims in 1291. King Philip the Fair of France, with an eye on the Templars' wealth, successfully obtained Pope Clement v's suppression of the Templar Order in 1312. At that time Templars' property passed into the hands of the other military order, the Hospitaller Order of St John of Jerusalem.

So from 1312 the Knights Hospitaller of St John acquired Templars' property in the Leswalt area of the Rhins, as well as in other parts of Scotland. The property in the Leswalt area was recorded as Craichmore, 'a certain croft, the Templeland, commonly called the Spital of Craighmore (or Creachmor)', which was rented in 1483 to Thomas McDowell by Sir William (Knollis) Knolys, Preceptor of the Order of St John (ibid, 175). Such 'spitals' were hospices. So it may be the case that such a hospice was founded and run by the Knights Hospitallers of St John in the vicinity of Craichmore or Hillhead of Craichmore steadings.

Whether or not the Knights Templars or Hospitallers were linked to the parish church in Leswalt is unknown.

As mentioned earlier, Leswalt Church had been transferred from the Diocese of Galloway to the jurisdiction of the Premonstratensian Canons of Tongland Abbey as early as 1355 to 1359. Thus it continued until the time of Henry Wemyss, who was Bishop of Galloway from 1526 to 1541. He evidently was in possession of Tongland Abbey by 1531, and in 1536 and 1541 the abbey was described as 'perpetually annexed' to the See of Galloway. Hence, sometime between 1526 and 1531 Leswalt Church once again came directly under the jursidiction of the Bishop of Galloway.

A charter (ibid, 31), dated 12 April 1537, granted the teinds and fruits of the parsonage of the kirk of Leswalt to Gilbert, earl of Cassillis and his heirs for 19 years, with the condition that they 'uphold the choir of the church in *thatch* and glass and other necessary ornaments to the high altar except silk and silver work.' A quite contemporary charter (ibid, 34), dated 11 July 1549, issued by the canons of the abbey of Whithorn, assigned to Alexander Vaus of Barnbarroch the parsonage and teind sheaves of the kirk of Longcaster [Longcastle] for 19 years. 'Alexander is to theik [roof] the queyr [choir or chancel] of the said kirk with *slaites* and shall uphold the kirk at the hands of the bishop.' Parish churches of this period obviously differed in their style of roofing, thatch or slate both being in use.

Thomas Melville, a secular priest, who had been vicar perpetual of Leswalt parish church, died before 1 January 1560 (z, 160).

William MacDowell was the priest vicar of the Leswalt Parish Church in 1559-60, just before the Reformation. Earlier in his priestly career he carried out chaplaincy work in 1554 at the Palace of Holyrood, and from 1554 was master of works to the Queen. After the Reformation he is recorded as vicar of Leswalt and Inch from 1561 to 1572, and died before 1580 (o, 56).

Thomas Alexander was reader in 1563, 1567 and exhorter in 1568-69. John Gibson (minister of Clayshant) had oversight of this church in 1574 (ibid, 160).

The parish church was taken over at the Reformation in 1560 and continued to be used for Presbyterian services up to 1828, when the nearby new parish church was built.

The roofless ruins of the original pre-Reformation church stand within the walled burial ground towards the west-end of Leswalt village. Because of pillage and ruination it is not possible to date the church's origin. But the remaining parts of the walls provide a good sense of its shape, size and structure. The rectangular church lies on an east-west axis, as is the case with most early churches. Two additions have been made to the original church: the eastern end has had a burial-vault added to it; and on the northern side a rectangular wing was added in the 17th century by the Agnew family. This wing probably had a gallery above and a burial-vault below, and has been entered by a plain, flat, lintelled door on its north wall. On the wall above the door is a four compartment window, with stone mullion and transom. A panel below the window shows that the wing was used as a burial-vault, as it contains an inscription and two coats of arms. The inscription states that it is in memory of Patritus Agnew of Lochnaw, Earl of Wigtown, and Margaret Kennedy, his wife, and dated 1644. The arms on the shields beneath are those of the Agnew and Kennedy families.

The church measures 12.8 metres by 4.5 metres within walls 0.8 metre thick and 2.4 metres high, and has been shortened, by the insertion of the east gable vault, from about 18.2 metres. The south wall incorporates an arched doorway and has three window-openings. The Agnew Wing measures 4.5 metres by 4.4 metres within walls 0.8 metre thick and 2.4 metres high.

On ceasing to be used as a church in 1828, the building was used for a time as the parish school, which seemingly accounts for a fireplace being still visible in the east wall of the church.

In 1916, a lady, reflecting on a visit to the area, writes:

> From the Craichmores, with their memory of Templars, lies the way to the village of Leswalt, and a little further are the ruins of the old church and its burial-ground. These ivy-covered and beautifully kept ruins are approached by a pathway with Irish yews on either side. The girdle of fine old sycamore trees, which enclose the whole, makes a charming setting. (s, 26/27)

Eighty years on, the ivy still clings to the ruins, the churchyard grass is cut, but, sad to say, the Irish yews have gone. There are still a few sycamore trees on two sides of the area, the interior of the roofless church ruins is thickly overrun with weeds and nettles, the churchyard gates have a warning notice about the unsafe state of the ruins, yet children do gain access and sometimes play in the area. So, today, it remains hallowed ground, a precious ruin, but, alas, largely neglected. The ruins require stabilisation and maintenance. It deserves such care.

Access: *OS Map Ref NX 0157 6385*

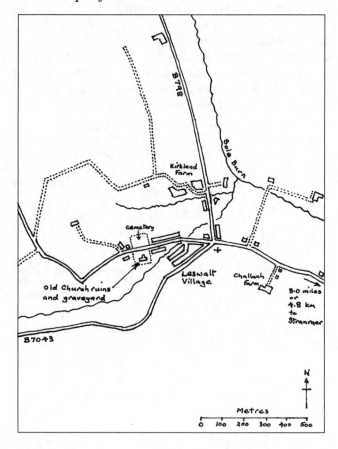

Its location is towards the western end of Leswalt village. On the gateway into the churchyard there is a warning about the dangerous state of the ruined church building. Hopefully, this will be attended to in the near future, to allow the public safe access to this historic Christian site.

St Mary's Chapel, Kilmorie

St Mary's Croft. Site of St Mary's Chapel, Kilmorie, in foreground.

On the east side of the northern Rhins, by Wig Bay, there is a farm called St Mary's Croft. 'In feudal days the croft tenant, if asked only, was to pay his superior lord one penny Scots money on the Feast of Candlemas' (s, 33-4). The farm is so called because on this site there stood for many centuries a little church or chapel dedicated to Our Lady. It was called Kilmorie, derived from the Gaelic *cill Moire*, the church of Mary. The date of erection of this little church is not known, but it is most likely to have been between the 7th and the 11th century. The 1908 edition of the Ordnance Survey map (Scale ½2500) shows the site of the church to be in the southern field in front of the farm building.

The little church may not have survived beyond the time of the Reformation. Timothy Pont's survey of the area in *c.* 1595 was used by John Blaeu in the production of his 1654 Map of Galloway, and this did not include Kilmorie. Symson (G, 62) writing in 1684, says: 'There was of old a chapel called Killemorie, but now wholly ruinous, within a little croft.'

In 1854, The Imperial Gazetteer of Scotland records that in the parish of Kirkcolm, on the shore of Loch Ryan, are vestiges of an ancient chapel dedicated to the Virgin Mary, and called Kilmorie, the Church of Mary (R, 246).

McKerlie (H, II, 193) writes in 1877, 'the ruins of the chapel in this parish are now believed to be in dykes.' Scott (Y, II, 338) also states that this St Mary's Chapel had stood at Kilmorie in the parish of Kirkcolm.

No remains of the little church are *in situ* today. All that can be seen at the site is a farm meadow. Although there is no indication of it being so, this meadow will probably conceal a centuries-old graveyard, since it would be appropriate to have burials in such hallowed ground.

The present farm steading continues to retain the title of St Mary's Croft.

At the south end of the Croft there is an ancient covered well, St Mary's Well. Of this, Symson (G, 62) writes in 1684, 'At the side of this Chapel, in the croft…there is a well, to which people superstitiously resort, to fetch water for sick persons to drink.' The covering stone slab is said to have been inscribed with lettering, but worn too smooth to be deciphered.

Access: *OS Map Ref NX 0339 6583*

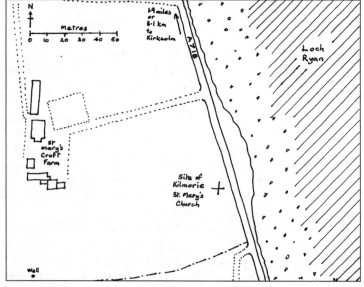

St Mary's Croft lies on the A718 road, some 3 kilometres south of Kirkcolm on Wig Bay. There is parking space at the side of the road. There are no remains of St Mary's Chapel. The site is private property of St Mary's Croft farm.

The Kilmorie Stone

History

This historic religious stone Cross is now lodged prominently in the churchyard of Ervie-Kirkcolm Parish Church. Its original site was at Kilmorie, on Wig Bay.

The Kilmorie Stone has not been accurately dated, but it probably dates from the 8th to the 10th century. As described in the section dealing with Clayshant, it may be a stone Cross originally erected in the 8th century Northumbrian period at the site of a 'field church', a burial-ground and a meeting place for prayer. Bishop or priest would make a visit from time to time for baptisms, burials and Mass. By early medieval times a stone-built chapel, dedicated to Our Lady, was erected at Kilmorie, which is the present-day site of St Mary's Croft farm. Given the state of preservation of the Kilmorie Stone, it may be that it was kept inside the chapel. Over a period of 800 to 1,000 years, from about the 8th century until the early 18th century, this ancient stone Cross stood at Kilmorie. Although the chapel was ruinous by the late 17th century, the stone Cross apparently remained at the site.

It is known that about 1720 the Kilmorie Stone Cross was taken to the nearby village of Kirkcolm, at which time the old medieval Church of St Columba was being repaired. The stone Cross was then treated as a building artefact and utilised as a lintel above the main western doorway of the renovated St Columba's Church. There it remained for a century, until 1821, when the old church was dismantled. It was then left lying in the grass. The old church site was within the confines of the Corsewall Estate. The old stone Cross was brought to the attention of Mr Carrick Moore, who arranged for it to be transferred and erected in the grounds of Corsewall House, beautifying its placement there with a fine ornamental garden.

Over the next century and more, the area surrounding the stone was encroached by overshadowing trees. During the winter of 1986-87 one large tree fell across the stone, but, fortunately, the latter sustained no damage because of the protection of the fallen tree's heavy branches. With permission from the owners of Corsewall Estate, the stone Cross was transferred in 1988 to its present site in the grounds of the Ervie-Kirkcolm Parish Church.

The Kilmorie Stone

Front   *Back*

Inscription

The stone is of a grey undressed whinstone type, with sculpturing on its front and back.

FRONT

The quality of the engraving and design on this face of the stone is far superior to that on the back, which it probably pre-dates. The engraving occupies the full length of the stone. The top third of the design consists of a sculptured Celtic-styled Cross. In its centre is an engraved circle, hollowed in the middle, which is taken to be a Eucharistic Host. It may just be construed as resting on a chalice. Around the Host and occupying the interior space of the Cross are tendrils.

The Cross surmounts an engraved shield which occupies the central section of this face of the stone. The shield has a horizontal bar, to the right of which is a small engraved cross. The central part of the shield has a second horizontal bar. And centrally set in the lower two-thirds of this shield is a stylized engraving which could be an animal, perhaps a lamb.

The lower part of this side is of an oblong shape containing an intricate engraving of serpents.

The general theme of this front face of the stone is that of good overcoming evil. The Cross of Christ victoriously poised above a shield which may portray the Lamb of God, the sacrificial price of the victory over the lower serpents representing evil.

BACK

The inferior engraving of this side though defined at the top is less clear below, and in its lower quarter may even have suffered some accretional disfigurement. The general pattern of the back, however, complements the front face.

The upper half again has an engraved outline of a Celtic Cross. It is surmounted by a simplistic figure of Christ, perhaps robed, with outstretched arms.

The lower half has some recognisable features, which have been interpreted in two ways.

1. McKerlie, in 1877, describing this side of the stone says:

> ...at the top is the crucifixion, and below this a man, having on one side of him two birds; on the other a pincers and two oblong objects,

which may be dice; all symbols of the passion. The figures are incises, and in the lowest style of design and execution.

2. An alternative interpretation is given by those who ascribe to this a Viking influence. The Cross is seen as surmounting a figure from Norse mythology.

The lower figure could be Odin with his two ravens 'Thought' and 'Memory'.

Alternatively the figure could be Sigurd, who according to the legend was a blacksmith, which could be denoted by the tongs. The legend also relates that he mastered the language of the birds and was warned by them of a plot against his life.

If either of these two Viking intepretations is correct, then the general message of this side of the stone is of the triumph of the Divine Christ over the pagan gods.

It is interesting to compare the front and back sculptures of the Kilmorie Stone. The two complementary Celtic-styled Crosses on either side have differing figurative inlays. Superimposed centrally on the front Cross is what can be construed as a Eucharistic Host, possibly surmounting a chalice. Superimposed on the rear Cross is an actual figure of Christ. Such an identical configuration of these two mirrored images is a very powerful and eloquent expression of Catholic Faith, then and now, of the Real Presence of Our Lord in the Eucharistic elements. How precious, in the Rhins, to have such an ancient, wonderful memorial, so expressively exclaiming in the silence of its stone the Faith that 'The Word was made flesh' (John 1:14) and 'This is my body. This is my blood.' (Mark 14:22, 24).

General

Comparison of photographs of the Kilmorie Stone taken near the beginning of this century and now, near the end of the century, shows a marked deterioration in the clarity of the engraving. It would seem that weathering has brought about withering and erosion of parts of the stone, rendering some of the engraving less clearly defined. The extent of this deterioration is a matter of concern. Within the space of this one century the stone has suffered more sculptural degradation than in the course of its previous thousand years of existence. Exposure, too, may account for all the splotch marks, which may be lichen or fungal growths, that have appeared on both faces of the stone since the beginning of this century. There is an awareness of the problem and a solution will be found to preserve this precious part of our Christian heritage.

Access to the Kilmorie Stone: *OS Map Ref NX 0270 6865*

Cars may be parked on the roadway outside the Ervie-Kirkcolm Parish Church in Kirkcolm. The entrance gate to the churchyard has a short path leading to the church. Presently, outside and to the right (east) side of the church, mounted on a rough plinth, is the Kilmorie Stone.

Killiecuddican

A chapel here is mentioned by Scott (Y, II, 338) as being one of the four chapels lying within the parish of Kirkcolm. He states that this chapel at Killiecuddican was dedicated to St Cuthbert, and that it was in the parish of Kirkcolm.

The Pont-Blaeu (1654), Roy (*c.* 1747) and Ainslie (1782) maps do not denote this chapel or place. This may not be very telling, because of a lack of minor features in their maps, or perhaps because the chapel may have ceased to exist by the time these maps were made. Symson, writing in 1684, makes no reference to this chapel, but this does not exclude the possibility of its former existence.

In the Ordnance Survey maps of 1850 (6 inches to 1 mile) and 1908 (large scale ½500) the area north of Ervie in the North Rhins is denoted as Killiemucuddican. This gives some corroboration to Scott's statement that there was a chapel at Killiecuddican.

There are no remains of this chapel, nor is its location known. But the persistence of the district name 'Killiemacuddican' gives grounds for credibility. The composite word 'Killiemacuddican' probably has a three-fold construction from the Gaelic. *Cille* means cell or chapel. The syllable *mo* is often prefixed to the names of Celtic period saints; this has honorific significance since *mo* means 'my'. The *mo* can become *ma. Cuddican* is a possible corruption of Cuthbert. An indication of this type of derivation is shown in the town name of Kirkcudbright, in Galloway. The *cudbright* part of this name is certainly a derivative of the name Cuthbert. It is of interest to note here the importance and the esteem in which St Cuthbert was held, in that not only were churches named after him, but a town, and, indeed, a county, Kirkcudbrightshire — the only county in Scotland to be named after a saint. MacQueen (Q2, 30) points out too that the South Ayrshire coastal village of Ballantrae was formerly called Kirkcudbright Innertigh, the new name being first recorded as late as 1617.

Why is St Cuthbert so important? Mostly, if not entirely, the answer to this question lies in his holiness.

The name Cuthbert comes from Saxon and not Celtic origins. It is said St Cuthbert was born *c.* 636 in the Lowlands of Scotland.

According to Bede, he was a Briton. During his youth he was a shepherd, before entering the monastic life at Melrose. In 661, when the monastery at Ripon was founded, Cuthbert was sent there as guest-master. Soon, he returned to Melrose, where he became prior. To assist people stricken with plague and to revive Christianity, he engaged in widespread missionary activity, which seemed to include parts of Galloway. His memory is perpetuated in Kirkcudbright, where a church, then the town, and as mentioned earlier, the county, were named after him. Disputes between the Celtic and Roman traditions over the date of Easter were resolved at the Council of Whitby in 664 in favour of the latter. While this was still a contentious issue, St Cuthbert was transferred to Lindisfarne, the Holy Isle, in Northumbria, now under the new Benedictine observance, where he fulfilled the role of prior. He won community respect and conformity by his holiness. At the same time he continued his missionary work. In 676 he sought greater closeness to God in a life of solitude, living as a hermit on a nearby desolate island of the Farne group. On Easter Day 685, at the personal request of King Egfrid, St Cuthbert was ordained as abbot-bishop of Lindisfarne by St Theodore at York. After his death in 687, his body was found to be incorrupt. Viking raids ended monastic life on Lindisfarne in 875; St Cuthbert's body was removed by the monks and transported across England until it reached Durham in 995. His shrine in Durham Cathedral was desecrated and plundered in the 16th century, during the reign of Henry VIII. St Cuthbert's relics were re-buried by the monks in the cathedral. In 1828, a further examination of his remains took place and the pectoral cross, vestments and ancient coffin were removed and may still be seen at Durham. The veneration of this great saint attests to his influence and the holiness of his life.

It would not be surprising to find St Cuthbert's name commemorated in the Rhins area of Galloway.

In Scott's later edition in 1950 (Y, VIII, 189) there is a change of mind about the dedication of this chapel. It then states, 'The chapel at Killiemaccudican was dedicated to St Mochuter, the name being Cill-Mo-Chudagon, Mochutu's Church, Mochester of Rathan and Lismore, who died in 637' quoting Maxwell Monuments, 13; Book of Caerlaverock, ii, 417; Watson's *Celtic Place Names*, 166.

MacQueen (Q2, 20) supports this dedication. He says that Killiemacuddican means 'my little Cutu's church', adding that St Muchutu of Rathan and Lismore is said to have died in 637. He also says that the parish church of Wigtown [*ecclesia S. Macuti*] is probably dedicated to the same saint.

St Mochuda, otherwise known as Carthage or Carthach the Younger, appears to have adopted the name of his master, St Carthach the Elder, who for his part called his disciple Mochuda, 'my Cuda' — Cuda being presumably the younger man's actual name. Mochuda was born in Kerry. On growing up, he followed a religious way of life. By the advice of St Colman Elo, with whom he made some stay, he decided to establish himself at Rathan in Offaly. He was abbot-bishop of the monastery he founded there, gradually assembling a large community of monks, for which he wrote a monastic rule. Shortly before his death he and his community were expelled. He led his monks to the banks of the Blackwater and there established the monastery school of Lismore. (I, 111-2) & (J, II, 306-7).

The chapel dedicated to St Cuthbert or St Mochuda at Killiecuddican could date from between the 8th and 12th centuries. If it survived to the Reformation in 1560, then it cannot have survived much longer since it is not chronicled nor shown in 17th- or 18th-century maps.

Access: *OS Map Ref NW c00 68*

The area straddles the B738 road between Ervie and Drumdow. There is no exact site, nor remains.

Chapel Donnan, Balsarroch

The site of Chapel Donnan lies in the field beyond the gate. Drumdow Farm is in the background.

St Donnan was an Irish monk of Iona under St Columba. Afterwards he became the abbot-founder of a monastery on the Island of Eigg in the Inner Hebrides. He and his fifty-two monk companions were massacred by heathen raiders on Easter Sunday in the year 618.

Several places and churches in Scotland are named after St Donnan. In the Rhins there is a Kildonan area and a Kildonan Burn, near Stoneykirk. There is a Dounan (Donnan) Bay on the west coast of the northern Rhins. Three chapels were dedicated to the saint in the Rhins: Chapel Donnan at Balsarroch in the northern Rhins; Kildonan Chapel, near Drummore; and Kildonan Chapel near Stoneykirk in the southern Rhins. It is likely that these chapels would have been erected sometime after the establishment of the Church of St Columba at Kirkcolm. It is not possible to be more precise than to say that these chapels dedicated to St Donnan were built sometime between the 7th and 11th centuries.

Scott (Y, II, 353) affirms that there was a St Donan's Chapel at Kildonan, in the parish of Kirkcolm.

On the site of Chapel Donnan in the North Rhins, two sculptured stone cross-slabs were found. One is part of a slab of sandstone 28cm high by 23cm wide and 5cm thick, sculptured on one face with an incised cross of Maltese form. The second is an irregular, quadrangular-shaped block of sandstone, 25cm high by 13cm wide and 8cm thick, sculptured on two faces with faintly incised crosses of Maltese form. These two stones are now in the National Museum of Antiquities in Edinburgh.

Nothing remains today of Chapel Donnan, but its location is shown as south-east of Broom Hill and east-north-east of Balsarroch in the (6 inches to the mile) 1850 edition of the Ordnance Survey map of the Rhins area. It is located more precisely in the (½2500 scale) Ordnance Survey map, 1908 edition.

On speaking to the local farmer, he revealed that when tilling the area it is noticeable that the soil appearance at the site of St Donnan's Chapel differs from that of its immediate surroundings. There are dry-stone walls at the edge of the field and additional deposits of other loose stones, but no visible foundational remains of the chapel.

It is likely that the chapel would be the site of a burial-ground.

Balsarroch

About 500 metres west of the site of Chapel Donnan are the remains of Balsarroch residence and farm. Records of this property go back to at least 1590. It would seem to have been landed property before the Reformation, the farm forming part of the old Corsewall barony. By the beginning of the 18th century it had passed into the hands of the Ross family. In 1768 Mr Andrew Ross, Presbyterian minister at Inch Church, and his wife were feudal holders of the property. It is said that their fourth child, John, was born while they were at Balsarroch. This child grew up to be Rear-Admiral Sir John Ross, famous for his two explorations of the Canadian Arctic area in unsuccessful attempts to find the North West Passage.

On a rise, some 250 metres south-east of Balsarroch is the Marian Tower monument. This is reputed to be the spot where Sir John's wife, Lady Marian Ross, would watch for her husband's return.

Access to Chapel Donnan site: *OS Map Ref NW 9983 6919*

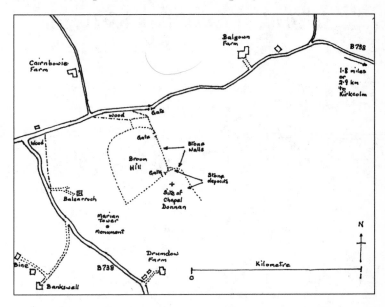

On the B738 road, little more than half a kilometre south-west of Balgown Farm, there is a field gate on the south side of the road. From here proceed on foot for approximately 450 metres southwards. The Chapel Donnan site is on private farm land, and is not presently marked or sign-posted. There are no remains.

St Bride's Chapel, East Kirkbryde

Ruins at the site of St Bride's Chapel, with East Kirkbryde farm buildings in the background.

St Brigid, also known as Bridget, Bride or Ffraid, was born at Faughart, near Dundalk. She founded the first nuns' convent in Ireland, at Kildare. Her great devotion seems to have been to the poor. She is a greatly venerated saint, and patron of Ireland after St Patrick. Her life spanned the years *c.* 450 to *c.* 525.

The Catholicism of the Celtic Church which spread throughout Scotland during and after St Columba's Iona missionary apostolate, brought with it a knowledge of, and a devotion to, St Brigid. This is witnessed to by the number of places and churches named after her and dedicated to her patronage. In England, for example, nineteen known pre-Reformation churches were dedicated to her (J, I, 229). In Scotland there is evidence of widespread devotion, with so many place names and chapels dedicated to her.

In the Rhins, there are the remains of two pre-Reformation chapels — one in the North Rhins, the other in the South Rhins.

In the far North Rhins, there are the two Kirkbryde Farms. West Kirkbryde is inhabited, East Kirkbryde is not occupied but used as a farm store. In the field just to the east of East Kirkbryde there is a mound of stones, running in an east-west direction for about 15 metres. These are the remains and this is the site of St Brigid's (Bride's) Chapel, one of the many Celtic chapels in the Rhins. It was built probably sometime between the 7th and the 11th centuries. Though not ruling this out, MacQueen (Q2, 25) considers it might date from any period of the Middle Ages. It seems to have survived after the 16th-century Reformation. It is not included in the Pont/Gordon Galloway map of 1654. Kirkbryde is mentioned as a place in Roy's map of *c.* 1747. Johnson, in his 1826 map, records East Kirkbride, but no church is indicated.

In a report (L, III) in 1841 it states:

> About a mile from Corsewall Castle, on a farm called Kirkbride, there was once a church dedicated to St Bride. Its foundations may still be traced. A part of the churchyard wall forms the side of a cottage. A tenant on the adjoining land remembers that, forty years ago, he dug up decayed pieces of coffins, with the iron handles, skulls, and other bones. The site was evidently chosen from the proximity of a well of remarkably pure water, which never fails in the driest seasons.

McKerlie (1877) writes about a chapel dedicated to St Bridget being here, remarking that the site alone remains, and is at East Kirkbride. When the chapel fell into dereliction is difficult to determine with accuracy.

Scott (Y, II, 338) affirms that there was a St Bride's Chapel at Kirkbride, in the parish of Kirkcolm.

Another Mckerlie (s, 33) writing in 1916 about this chapel at Kirkbryde, says: 'It is possible there was a conventual establishment here dedicated to St Brigid.'

Perhaps not unrelated to this is a nearby location. On the west side of Loch Ryan, some 2.5 kilometres north-east of Kirkbryde, there is Lady Bay. Ainslie's 1782 map names it Port More — More probably derived from the Gaelic *Moire* for Mary and therefore named after Our Lady. At the top of the track leading down to the bay is the farm of Portencalzie (pronounced Portencally or Portencailly). The Pont-Blaeu map of 1654 names it Portinkailly, while Ainslie's map of 1782 names it Portencally. McKerlie (H, II,196) says that the Gaelic-based name Poirtinkailly has been translated as 'port in the wood', but he considers that, since the suffix for the name of the bay has a religious connotation, likewise the Poirtinkailly suffix is more likely to be derived from *cilly* (pronounced killy) for a chapel, relating to one at or near the haven. He adds that another opinion has it as being from

Portan Cailleach, port of the nuns. Whether the suffix refers to a chapel or to nuns, it would seem to refer to the nearby chapel dedicated to St Brigid located at East Kirkbryde. This may give just a little support to the suggestion of a conventual establishment also at that site.

The immediate area around the chapel was a burial-ground, as indicated earlier. Presently there is no surface evidence of this, e.g. no gravestones. Whether indicative or not, around July time, ox-eye daisies proliferate on the north side of the remaining chapel ruins.

McKerlie (H, II, 194) also mentions the existence of St Bride's Well near the chapel site. This is shown in the Ordnance Survey map, 1908 edition (scale ½2500). Its location is south-west of East Kirkbryde Farm and south-west of St Brigid's Chapel site.

Access: *OS Map Ref NX 005 708*

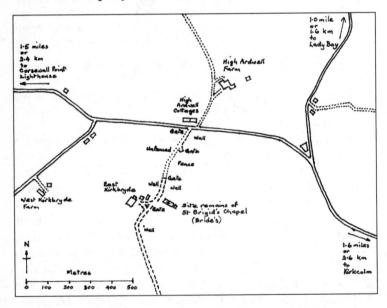

From the junction of the A718 and B738 roads, take the unnumbered road leading to Corsewall Point. On the right-hand side, 1.5 kilometres along this minor road, are the High Ardwell cottages. Opposite the cottages there is a gate and a path. Walk along this path for some 300 metres and East Kirkbryde farm buildings are to the right (west side of path) and the site-remains of St Brigid's Chapel to the left (east side of the path).

Topmalloch

Topmalloch lies in the southern part of Lochnaw Castle estate. On the east side of the Green Burn and some 300 metres north-west of Blackpark Farm is Topmalloch Hill. Sir Andrew Agnew (w, 178) states that a chapel, built by St Malachy, was situated in this area. He adds that the chapel had no rath. (A rath is described as a circular earthwork, a defensive homestead or settlement). Topmalloch Hill and, to its east, Topmalloch Wood are derived from the saint's name.

St Malachy (1095-1148), a reforming Bishop of Down, seems to have journeyed through Galloway more than once *en route* to Rome. He is associated with the foundation of Soulseat Abbey. If the chapel at Topmalloch is also associated with him, then it would have been built in the 12th century. Sir Andrew Agnew (h, i, 101) conjectures that the ancient castle of Lochnaw, which was situated on an island at the loch, was also built in the 12th century. So there may have been a link between the origin of the castle and of the chapel.

There is no physical evidence today of the chapel. However, within Lochnaw Castle estate, on the south-west side of Topmalloch Hill, there lies, by the south side of the Green Burn, the ruin of an old cottage. In the Ordnance Survey (2½ inches to the mile) map of 1959, this cottage is named as Ochteralinachan. It is similarly named in the 1850 edition (6 inches to the mile). This shows about five buildings in this area by the Green Burn, and also Blackpark Farm to the south. No indication is given of a chapel. Ochteralinachan lies on a north-west/south-east axis. It seems to be the only remains of a building in the area. Accepting that at one time a chapel was situated here, it just may be that this ruined cottage was converted out of the old chapel.

Access *OS Map Ref NW c987 618*

To reach this ruin, entry is made from the B738 road via Larbrax Lodge on the south-west side of Lochnaw Castle estate. About 100 metres along the estate lane the Green Burn crosses under the lane. A footpath to the right follows the burn on its south side. This is a lovely walk through the wood, with an abundance of ferns, wild flowers and some rhododendrons. After some 400 metres, the path ends. The ruins are nearby and can be approached through the obscuring trees to the left.

Cairnhapple

The Pont-Blaeu map of 1654 shows Karn chaple on the west side of the north Rhins, situated near the coast and westwards of Lochnaw.

In Ainslie's 1782 map, the same location, shown as a hill, is named Drumawhirn. He shows Cairnhapple as a building on the road, two-thirds the way from Galdenoch and one-third the way from Lochnaw.

McKerlie (H, II, 189) writing about this place, refers to it as 'Cairnhapple, which is a corruption for Chapel in the suffix, pointing to some place of worship not now known.'

In William Johnston's 1826 map of Wigtownshire, he shows Cairnhapple as a building on the north side of the road from Lochnaw to Little Galdenoch and Knocknain.

The more detailed 1850 Ordnance Survey (6 inches to the mile) map shows Cairnhapple as a building on the southern slope of Cairnhapple Hill and east of the south-east corner of Lochnaw Loch. It is on the east side of the road running southwards to Portpatrick. The lesser road, passing Cairnhapple, crosses the Portpatrick road and goes via Smith's Croft to Meikle Galdenoch. This is replicated in the 1856 Ordnance Survey (one inch to the mile) map.

Apart from the suggestion coming from the name, there is no evidence of a chapel or its remains at Cairnhapple.

Access:

OS Map Ref NW c 965 645, or NW c983 635 or NW c985 628

East of Rhins

Glenluce Abbey

Glenluce Parish Church

St John's Chapel, Knock of Luce

KirkChrist Chapel, Milton

Our Lady's Chapel, Balcarry

St Fillan's Chapel, Kilfillan

Kilfeddarr

Kilmacfadzean

Kilgallioch

Glenluce Abbey

United in their Christian life within the Catholic Church there are many kinds of religious families or communities. St Benedict in the early 6th century developed a Rule for monastic life. During the 8th and 9th centuries this Benedictine form of monasticism, with the support of the Carolingian kings, overtook other forms and it became the norm for western monasticism. In the 10th and 11th centuries, many monasteries were reformed. The Abbey of Cluny, in France, came to prominence and influence in this period. In 1098, Abbot Robert of Molesme failed to persuade the monks of his house to adopt a more austere form of the Benedictine life, as it had evolved. With 21 of his monks he founded a new monastery at Citeaux, in Burgundy. This enterprise was failing, when, in 1112, a 22-year-old Burgundian noble named Bernard (1090-1153) joined the community. He was the force that launched the Cistercian (named after Citeaux) Order on its period of impressive growth. By 1200 there were 525 Cistercian houses or abbeys all across Christendom. In 1500, the Order had 738 houses of men and about 650 houses of women (P2, 201).

St Benedict, St Robert and St Bernard played their part in the family life of the Church. It was into this evolved Cistercian monastic community that Glenluce Abbey came into being. The abbey was founded in 1190/1/2 (on 21 January, 1192, according to Reid (ᴋ, 37)), by Roland, Lord of Galloway and Constable of Scotland. As was the Cistercian custom, a new abbot with twelve monks came from an existing monastery to found the new abbey. Glenluce was originally staffed with monks from Dundrennan (cf. ʙ, 75). In 1192, Glenluce was the sixth Cistercian monastery to be established in Scotland. By that date, too, there were also six Cistercian communities of nuns in Scotland (ʙ, 72 & 144). In the Solway area, Dundrennan Abbey, near Kirkcudbright, had earlier been established by King David ɪ in 1142. There is also the suggestion that Cistercians were established at Soulseat for a short period in the 1140s, by St Malachy. It was at Melrose in 1136 that King David ɪ had introduced the Order into Scotland.

The Cistercian, enclosed, monastic life is centred on the daily Mass and prayer, communal and private. This is coupled with a schedule of work, which ranges from farming, for which they have a very good reputation, to the many skills demanded of their way of life, including building, maintenance work, a full range of domestic work and other arts and crafts. Before printing came along, manuscripts and hand-made religious books would also be included in their range of work. Hospitality is also a feature of their religious life.

At the time of the establishment of Glenluce Abbey, there was already in the village of Glenluce a parish church. The latter, Cowan (ᴀ, 76) states, was 'undoubtedly annexed to the Abbey of Glenluce from its foundation in 1191/2, the abbey church may have been that of the parish.'

William, the first known abbot, may have been so from the inception of the abbey. He was still in office in 1216 (ᴋ, 38).

Reid (ibid, 38-9) says:

> By the statutes of the Order every abbot was bound to appear at the annual General Chapter at the Burgundian mother abbey of Citeaux held in September, where the heads of all abbeys from every corner of Christendom met in one of the most international and democratic assemblies in the Middle Ages. There they discussed as equals, judged and were judged even in absentia. The Scottish abbots had the privilege of coming only every fourth year.

The Statutes of the Chapter General of the Cistercian Order were published at Louvain in 1933, edited by J Canivez in eight volumes. In the statutes of 1199 light is thrown on the relationship between Dundrennan and Glenluce *vis-à-vis* the foundation of the latter, and also on the organisational control exercised within the Order. In 1199, a year of strife in Galloway, Abbot William of Glenluce was due at Citeaux. Cowan (B, 75) comments:

> [The 1199 statutes] refer to the abbot of Dundrennan advising his 'son-abbot' to absent himself from the General Chapter, and to the abbot of Glenluce as, by the advice of his 'father', staying away from it, indicate that Glenluce was a daughter-house of Dundrennan.

Even so, this would be an autonomous relationship. Reid (K, 39), citing the same statute, adds that while he gave his fellow-abbot William at Glenluce this advice to stay at home,

> [the abbot of Dundrennan] himself braved the undoubted terrors of the journey. But his brother abbots took a severe view of William's absence and ordained the abbot of Glenluce to fast every Friday on a single meal of bread and water till he returned to Citeaux the next year and till then was forbidden to enter his abbatial stall. The abbot of Dundrennan for his advice received eight days of light penance, one of which was to be on bread and water.

It is not known when Gilbert, who had been Master of Novices at Melrose, succeeded as abbot. He retired to Melrose, but clergy and people called for him to return as Bishop of Galloway. This was approved and he remained in possession of the See until his death in 1233 (ibid, 39).

The third abbot we know about at Glenluce was Robert. He seems to have imposed himself into this office. Reid (ibid, 39) describes him as

> Robert, the so-called abbot, mentioned in the *Chronicle de Mailros*, p. 147. Times were wild in Galloway and Alexander II was campaigning against Thomas, the illegitimate claimant to the province, and it would appear that someone — perhaps an interested outsider — aided Robert to intrude, and Jordan, abbot of Dundrennan, did not do his duty. But the General Chapter was alert and ordered in 1234 an investigation of the affair by the abbots of Rievaulx, Roche and Sawley, as unprejudiced outsiders. Not only was Robert removed, but Jordan was also deposed for his negligence.

It was in 1235 that the abbey was molested during the continuing rebellion in Galloway. Some of King Alexander II's soldiers 'more sons of the Devil than of Mars', took to plundering religious houses. At Glenluce, according to the *Chronicle de Mailros*, p. 145, they stripped a monk, who was dying on the floor of the infirmary on his traditional death-bed of ashes and straw, of the only sheets which covered him (ibid. 40).

Whether or not indicative of local stability and continuity, the history of the abbey is obscure between the mid-13th and the onset of the 16th century. During that period, Robert the Bruce visited Glenluce a few months before his death in 1329, and James IV visited the abbey twice when on pilgrimage to Whithorn.

Many other pilgrims would stop at Glenluce Abbey *en route* to Whithorn, which was a major pilgrimage centre from its inception in the late 4th century until the 16th-century Reformation period. Such pilgrimages have since then been resumed.

In the 15th century, near to Glenluce Village parish church, stood Ballinclauch, a residential area of importance. This is indicated by the issue on 27 January 1498/9, of a royal charter by James IV confirming free burgh in barony status to 'the vill of Ballinclauch, belonging to the monastery of Glenluce' (ibid, 58). This same charter throws some light on the integration of abbey and local community. Michael, the abbot, had appealed to have a fair, approved by previous charter, which was held annually on the Feast of the Nativity of the Virgin Mary (8 September) — 'because it could not be on that day well and easily, without grave damage and loss to the said abbot and convent and the lieges resorting to the same, in their harvests which are commonly at that time and which would be impeded by the fair' — changed to the day of the Feast of the Visitation of the Virgin Mary (31 May), considered more convenient. The charter gave approval for this change, and so the requirements of harvest and holiday and abbey and people were satisfied. McKerlie (s, 46) says 'Ballinclach was the name [of Glenluce Village] in the olden days, when the 'Nativity' or 'Mary Fair' was held there.'

From the 12th to the 16th century the Glenluce Abbey monks seemingly extended their farming, developing the land south of Glenluce village and east of the Water of Luce estuary. In this area they erected three chapels: Our Lady's at Balcarry, KirkChrist, and St John's at Knock of Luce. There may have been a fourth one, St Fillan's at Kilfillan. To the north of Glenluce Abbey there are two distant farms which may at one time have had chapels built by the monks, one at Kilfeddar and another at Kilmacfadzean.

In the 16th century the Glenluce Abbey community suffered considerable disturbance and spoliation. Disputes over the abbacy by a series of commendators were brought to an end by the provision of Walter Mallen as abbot on 13 June 1519. During his extended term of office the abbey regained some stability. It may have been in the late 15th century, or during Abbot Walter's period of office, that the rebuilding of the chapter-house took place. This chapter-house, with its beautiful stone-vaulted ceiling, is now the only remaining roofed part of the monastery ruins.

In 1544, Abbot Walter was expelled by the Earl of Cassillis; and in 1545-46 the abbey was invaded both by his followers and those of Gordon of Lochinvar, who sought possession of it. Walter Mallen then resigned in favour of James Gordon, brother of James (or John) Gordon of Lochinvar — this was on 5 December 1547. The titular James Gordon of Glenluce died before March, 1560, and Lochinvar occupied the abbey and expelled the monks.

A protégé of the Earl of Cassillis, Thomas Hay, who had been provided on 17 April 1560, was instituted as abbot on 29 September 1560, the institution taking place in the local village parish church, owing to the occupancy of the abbey. After temporary residence with his monks in Maybole, under the protection of Gilbert, Earl of Cassillis, and with the help of the latter's negotiation, Gordon relented and the monks resumed occupancy of Glenluce Abbey (cf. K, 44-55).

The Papal Bull, appointing Thomas Hay abbot, issued by Pope Pius IV in 1560

> sets forth the cares and anxieties of his Holiness for the setting up and government of churches and monasteries in all the world, and more particularly for the monastery of the Blessed Virgin Mary of the Valley of Light (Vallis Lucis), otherwise Glenluce, of the Cistercian Order, in the Diocese of Candida Casa. (H, I, 188)

The sentiments expressed in this Bull reflect the Church's concern and endeavour at that time. It was written during the great reforming Council of Trent, which was convened in 1545 and concluded, after three sessions, in 1563.

> [The Papal Bull of 1560 went further than merely the appointment of Abbot. The remaining abbacy lands were conveyed to Thomas Hay on the proviso that no addition should be made to the monks of Luce, and that, when all the existing residents were dead, he should inherit the lands. This was ratified by Queen Mary, and confirmed at the Reformation. Thomas Hay became an early convert to Protestantism, thereby ensuring the permanency of the gift. It is said he married a daughter of Kennedy of Bargany, and had issue. He was succeeded by his son, Thomas Hay of Park. (H, I, 189)

A charter signed also in 1560 by the abbot, prior, sub-prior and thirteen monks (one or two other monks, known at this time, did not sign the charter) gives some idea of the size of the Glenluce community at this time. Donaldson (o, 48), who has made a study of the Galloway clergy over the period of the Reformation, remarks of this group of Cistercian monks at Glenluce Abbey that 'not one appears as a minister, exhorter, or reader in the diocese of Galloway.' It would seem that John Sanderson was an exception, since the same source (ibid. 58) cites him variously as minister, exhorter and reader at Glenluce Parish Church after the Reformation.

For three and a half centuries the Cistercian monks of Glenluce Abbey played their part in the religious life of this area of Galloway. From the abbey's inception in 1190/1/2 it seems, from Cowan (A, 76), that it had become responsible for staffing the local village of Glenluce (Old Luce) with a priest for its parish church.

In 1572 the Abbot-Commendator and six monks were still resident at the abbey.

> The monastery was certainly heavily endowed with lands...lands which seem to have covered the whole parish of Glenluce, with some lands in the parishes of Inch and Kirkinner. They are detailed in a feu charter, granted by Thomas Hay, last abbot, to Gilbert, Earl of Cassillis, on 17 April 1572. For this feu the earl paid no less than £10,000 Scots and an annual feu duty of £666.13s.4d. (K, 37)

Thomas Hay, son of Abbot Thomas Hay, acquired the lands of Park, just south of the Glenluce Abbey site. In 1572 he married Janet McDowall of Garthland. He built the fortified House of Park, which is still in use today, and placed an inscription over the doorway, which reads: 'Blessit be the name of the Lord. This verk was begun the — day of March, 1590, be Thomas Hay of Park, and Jonet Makdoval, his spouse.' As Reid remarks (K, 37), 'So when the abbot's son set to work to build the House of Park he can have had no anxiety as to finance', considering the huge sum then, in excess of £10,000 Scots, acquired by his father on the sale of most of his property to the Earl of Cassillis in 1572.

Abbot Thomas Hay remained as commendator until his death in 1580. Gilbert Moncrief and Laurence Gordon followed him as commendators. By 1602 the last monk had passed away. In 1619 the abbey was bestowed on the Bishop of Galloway (B, 75). In 1641 the property was acquired for a manse and glebe.

MacGibbon and Ross (U, III, 133) state that:

> in this remote region the buildings remained long undisturbed, and as late as 1646 the abbey is referred to in the Records of the Presbytery of Stranraer as having received little injury.

Symson (G, 57), who wrote in 1684, states:

> The steeple and part of the walls of the church, together with the chapter-house, the walls of the cloister, the gatehouse with the walls of the large precincts, are for the most part yet standing.

Plundering of abbey stone for other buildings would seem to have taken place from the late 16th century. Over the centuries, much of the complex has been reduced to its foundations. What remains is well preserved and the general layout is easy to interpret. The abbey buildings have consisted of a cruciform church, with a cloister garth in the usual position to the south of the nave, and ranges of conventual buildings on the three remaining sides of the square with outlying buildings. Dormitories were above the ground floor of the east range, and for a time also above the ground floor of the west range, but the latter was remodelled to form part of the abbot's or commendator's house. The main survival is the south transept of the church and the east range of the cloister adjoining it. This latter range contains the extant chapter-house with its fine stone-vaulted roof. The south range of the cloister contained most of the domestic buidings — the kitchen, bakehouse, brewhouse, and refectory. Some fireplaces in these rooms survive. The building and design skills are everywhere to be seen. Partly exposed, one can still see the system of water conduits which carried water into and out of the abbey, providing drinking water and flushing the abbey drains.

In the north transept of the church there is a gravestone dedicated to Robert Gordon of Lochinvar, who died in 1548. In the south chancel wall there is a late 17th century armorial panel inset with the arms of Thomas Hay of Park and Janet Hamilton, his wife. In 1884, a fragment of a cross-slab, probably from the 11th century, was found within the chapter-house. This slab, which is now in the abbey museum, has the incised outline of a Greek cross with expanded terminals to the arms and ringed armpits. A second cross-slab (now lost), which is said to have been found incorporated in the masonry above the chapter-house, bore 'an incised cross in outline and two holes cut through'. This slab may originally have come from the site of a chapel, which is said to have stood at Back of the Wall. (D, 59)

Back o' Wall is a farm, adjacent to and on the south side of Glenluce Abbey. The chapel that is said to have stood there may have been a domestic or wayside chapel associated with the abbey; it may even have served the monks' purpose at some early stage in the setting up of the monastery in the late 12th century.

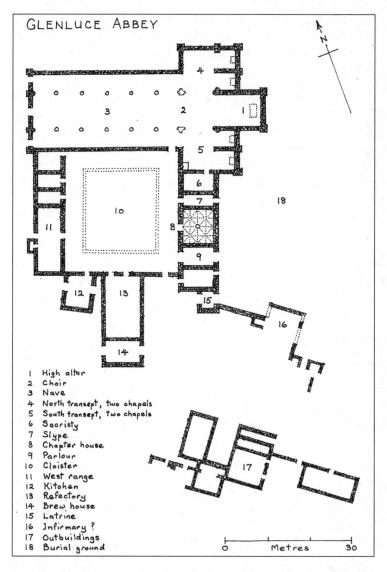

GLENLUCE ABBEY

1 High altar
2 Choir
3 Nave
4 North transept, two chapels
5 South transept, two chapels
6 Sacristy
7 Slype
8 Chapter house
9 Parlour
10 Cloister
11 West range
12 Kitchen
13 Refectory
14 Brew house
15 Latrine
16 Infirmary ?
17 Outbuildings
18 Burial ground

0   Metres   30

Since 1933, Glenluce Abbey ruins have come under State care. The Secretary of State for Scotland discharges this responsibility now through the agency of Historic Scotland. The remains of the abbey are beautifully maintained and provide a testimony to the dedication and skill of the Cistercian monks, whose building and farming expertise, prayer, work and service graced the area for over three and a half centuries. Their legacy of Christian life has entered into the religious culture and is an integral part of our inheritance.

List of Abbots

The Records and Charters of the Abbey, from which the names of the successive abbots could have been verified, have never been found. The names given in this incomplete list have been obtained from various sources not directly connected with the Abbey. (V, 140), (K, 38-55).

Date of Office		Names of Abbots
Source V	Source K	
1212	c. 1191	William
1235	1233	Gilbert (later Bishop of Galloway) (Died 1233 (K, 39))
1236	c. 1234	Robert
1243	1236-48	Michael
		was succeeded by Alan Musarde
		Then a silence for two centuries during which two names occur.
	c. 1347	Bede
	c. 1381	Adam
		then
1496	c. 1496-97	Michael
	c. 1500	Robert Betoun (Beaton) 1506 appointed Abbot of Melrose
	c. 1509	Dominico Grimani, Cardinal of St Mark, Patriarch of Aquileia and 'Protector of Scotland', Abbot 'in commendam'
		Quintin McCalbert
1514		Cuthbert Bailie
	c. 1513	Cardinal of Eusebius 'in commendam'
	c. 1513-19	David Hamilton, Bishop of Argyll, 'in commendam'
	c. 1515-16	Alexander Cunyngham
1517-45	c. 1519	Walter Malynne (Maclean), Malyning or Malin, Abbot for about 30 years
1547-48		Robert Gordon
1554-59	c. 1555	James Gordon
1559	1560-c. 1580	Thomas Hay
	1580-81	Gilbert Moncrief, Commendator
1581	1581	William Gordon (provisional appointment)
1584-1620	1581-1620	Lawrence Gordon, Commendator

The Abbey as an ecclesiastical institution came to an end at this last date (v, 140). The property was bestowed on the Bishop of Galloway in 1619. (B, 75)

Access: *OS Map Ref NX 1849 5867*

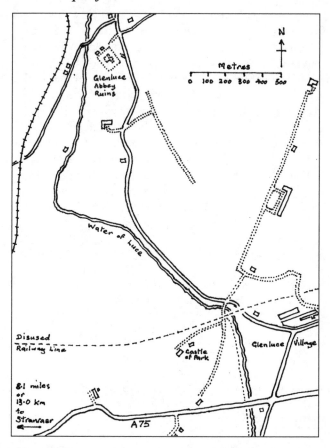

From the western end of Glenluce village, take the minor road northwards for 1.6 kilometres. The abbey ruins are on the left-hand (west) side of this road. There is a car park. The abbey grounds are open to the public, the times being seasonal, and a charge is made for admission.

Glenluce Parish Church

On a prominence near the centre of Glenluce village stands the present parish church, built in 1814. It stands within its walled burial-ground on the site of its predecessor, which is said to have been erected in 1637. On the south side of the church there are several 17th and 18th century gravestones. It is most probable that the original medieval Catholic church also stood on this site.

It would seem that this original parish church was founded in Glenluce (Old Luce) village prior to the establishment nearby of the Cistercian monks at Glenluce Abbey in 1190/1/2. The date of establishment may have been between the 8th and 11th centuries. Some evidence of the church's existence in that period is provided by a cross-slab of early medieval date, together with a number of others, which have been found within or in the vicinity of the church burial-ground.

A free-standing cross-slab from the site is now in the Royal Museum of Scotland (IB 45). It is carved in low relief and bears a Maltese cross above a vertical panel of complete interlace (eight-strand, median-incised plain plait) and a horizontal panel filled with a four-cord plait.

In the north wall of the church, to the east of the north transept, and now obscured by harling, there are fragments of two crosses, which probably date to the 11th century. One is part of a cross-head, which has a central boss and wedge-shaped arms incised with triquetra. The other shows part of the incised outline of a Greek cross within two concentric circles, and has a two-strand knot at the edge of the slab.

In 1935/36 the fragment of a cross-slab, now in the Royal Museum of Scotland (IB 239) was discovered in a wall about 183 metres north of the church. On both faces it has part of the incised outline of a Greek cross, which has a central boss, wedge-shaped arms and ringed armpits framed by a flat-band moulding. (D, 60)

Reid (K, 86) says that 'the church at Glenluce was dedicated to St Michael.' Scott (Y, VIII, 190) states this too.

Cowan (A, 76) states that the parish church was:

undoubtedly annexed to the abbey of Glenluce from its foundation in 1191/2, the abbey church may have been that of the parish. No vicarage existed in 1319, but while both parsonage and vicarage continued with the abbey at the Reformation, a vicar pensioner then served the cure, the position, however, normally being held by one of the monks.

Andrew Hannay was the priest curate of the parish on 12 March 1547. The Cistercian priest-monk, John Sanderson, of Glenluce Abbey, was fulfilling the parish priest's role as vicar pensioner on 16 May 1558. In the year of the Reformation it is recorded that he was still holding that office on 25 October 1560 (z, 100). In June 1563 he is styled 'minister' of Glenluce, and had been in possession of the croft and manse since at least 1562. He is recorded as exhorter in the parish from 1563 to 1572, and as reader, with a third of the vicarage, from 1567 to 1574. He is recorded as deceased in 1592/3 (o, 58). Mr James Fothinghame, possibly prebendary of Fowlis-Easter collegiate church, was minister in 1574 (z, 100).

An unusual installation service took place in this parish church in 1560. Thomas Hay was instituted as Abbot of Glenluce Abbey on 29 September 1560; the institution took place in the parish church, because the abbey at that time had been occupied by usurpers under the leadership of rival claimant, James Gordon of Lochinvar. In time, this dispute was settled.

As mentioned earlier, since the Reformation there have been two successive replacement churches on this site.

Access: *OS Map Ref NX 1965 5745*

The site is centrally located on a prominence in Glenluce village. No remains are visible of the medieval church, nor the replacement one of 1637. Only the church built in 1814 is on the site.

St John's Chapel, Knock of Luce

The field in the foreground is the site of St John's Chapel. Knock of Luce Farm and Hill are in the background.

Near and just north of an old track or road, leading from Machermore via Knock of Luce Farm to Kirkcowan, and shown in the Ordnance Survey map (scale ½2500, 1908 edition, there is the site of St John's Chapel.

This is one of a string of ancient chapels, which indicate an old route from Glenluce to Kirkcowan. These chapels include Our Lady's, near Balcarry, possibly St Fillan's at Kilfillan, Kirkchrist, near Milton, then St John's at Knock of Luce. Continuing north-westwards on this route for a further 5.2 kilometres, the Tarf water is reached, on the west side of which is Kenmure Farm. Just across the river, east of the farm, are the ruins of another ancient chapel. Thus, there were as many as five chapels on this old route between Glenluce and Kirkcowan. In the medieval period, Glenluce Abbey had possession of much of this area. The farm at Knock of Luce certainly belonged to Glenluce Abbey. Its name is included in a feu-charter list of abbey properties, transferred by the last abbot, Thomas Hay, to Gilbert, Earl of Cassillis, on 17 April 1572 (*Registrum Magni Sigilli* 1546/80-2, 202). Scott (Y, II, 347) states that St John's Chapel at Knock of Luce lay within the parish of Glenluce.

The site of St John's Chapel is about 170 metres east of Knock of Luce Farm. About 20 metres north-west of the chapel site is St John's Well.

The dedication of this chapel is either to St John, the apostle and evangelist, or to St John the Baptist; probably the former. The chapel may have been built by the Cistercian monks of Glenluce Abbey, some time after 1192, or it may be an earlier founded chapel taken over by the monks.

No clear outlined remains of the old chapel survive. In addition to a lengthened mound of unhewn stones, which are probably the gathered remains of the chapel, there are, round the slightly elevated central area of this chapel field, sections of stones protruding from the ground, as if to signify and reinforce the area within which the chapel was sited.

It is reported that three distinct paved floors, one above the other, were removed from these ruins (E, 129). McKerlie (S, 47) comments: 'The fact that three distinct paved floors superposed have been found in the ruins suggests interesting history of different periods.'

On the terrace at Lochinch Castle is a cross-slab which was found in 1907 on the farm of Knock of Luce, in cultivated land there called the Chapel Hill. The slab measures about 0.9 metre in length, is 16.5 cm in breadth at one end, tapering to 5.0 cm at the other, and is 10.0 cm in thickness. It is rudely carved in relief thus — at the broad end a cross of the Maltese form, measuring 21.5 cm by 15.0 cm; below it a compartment, containing in the upper portion a similar cross of smaller dimensions, and a single key pattern beneath, and at the base another single key pattern. E, 28)

At the chapel site near Knock of Luce Farm, St John's Well is still *in situ* and, although unused, continues to provide clear, fresh, drinking water. The stones surrounding the well are just above ground level, and at present there is a loose sheet of corrugated iron covering the well.

Access: *OS Map Ref NX 263 557*

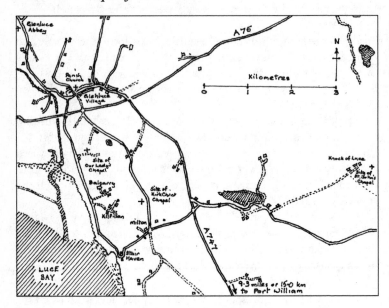

About 3.0 kilometres southwards on the A747 Glenluce to Port William road turn left (eastwards) via Whitefield Loch to Machermore Farm and along the farm track road to Knock of Luce Farm. The site of St John's Chapel is some 170 metres east of the farm.

KirkChrist Chapel, Milton

Site of KirkChrist Chapel in the field beyond foreground wall. Milton Farm in the central background. Luce Bay to the right.

This chapel was situated 530 metres north-north-west of Milton Farm, near Stair Haven, and 50 metres west of the Barnsallie Burn. The chapel is reported by McKerlie (H, I, 173) as belonging to Glenluce Abbey. Like other chapels in this area — Our Lady's, St John's, and perhaps one at Kilfillan — it may have been an early chapel taken over by the monks, or one built by the monks after the founding of Glenluce Abbey in *c.* 1192. Before the Reformation in the 16th century, all of the land in this area came under the jurisdiction of Glenluce Abbey.

Symson (G, 57), writing in 1684, says 'Middway betwixt Balcarrie and Schinnernes, and about halfe a mile from each, there is an old chapel or kirk, call'd Kirkchrist, but now it is ruinous.' Scott (Y, II, 347) also records the historical existence of this chapel called KirkChrist. Today there are no remains.

In Roy's map, *c.* 1747, he shows a number of buildings in the area and gives the name KirkChrist. In Ainslie's map of 1782 the same cluster of buildings is called Milltown.

In the 1908 Ordnance Survey map (scale ½500) KirkChrist Corn Mill is shown 70 metres north-west of South Milton farm. The Milton Burn, which runs beside both farm and corn mill, is shown in the same map being crossed by a bridge called KirkChrist Bridge, some 55 metres north-east of South Milton farm. Also shown is the Chapel Well, situated 335 metres south of the site of KirkChrist Chapel, by and on the east side of the Barnsallie Burn. The Clauchan Well or Lady Well is shown to the east side of the road running northwards from South Milton Farm, and 360 metres from KirkChrist Bridge. In 1908 a roadway ran north-westwards from near South Milton Farm to Kilfillan Farm, which is one kilometre away. It crossed the Milton Burn at the south side of its confluence with the Barnsallie Burn via the Kilfillan Bridge. This old road seems to have wound its way through Kilfillan and Balcarry to link up at Corsehead with the old medieval road from Glenluce to Whithorn. KirkChrist Chapel was on this latter route. This old main route from Glenluce southwards into the Machars is clearly shown in Ainslie's 1782 map.

So many places and objects in this area have Christian connotations. It seems that it was an extensive area in the southern part of Glenluce Abbey land and developed for farming by the monks or by feudal farmers. The field where KirkChrist Chapel stood is known as the Jerusalem Fey or Park (E, 129). This field was part of the property of Kilfillan Farm. The word 'fey' in Galloway means a croft or infield land.

In 1877, McKerlie (H, II, 228) wrote:

> At Cassendeoch there is a sculptured stone which was found in an old dyke about 1858. For eight years previously it was used as a step-stone to a pigstye. A portion of the sculpture forms a kind of St. Andrew's Cross. The description in full [is] given by the Rev G Wilson. The place where it was found is close to the site of KirkChrist Chapel, in the Jerusalem fey of Kilfillan.

Access: *OS Map Ref NX 213 550*

Halfway between Stair Haven and the A747 Glenluce to Port William road is the farm of Milton. From here, 0.7 kilometre northwards, the secondary road crosses the Barnsallie Burn. The chapel site is in the field to the west of the burn, about 120 metres from the bridge. There are no remains. (See previous section on St John's Chapel, Knock of Luce, for map.)

Our Lady's Chapel, Balcarry

View from Corsehead Farm, looking towards Luce Bay. Site of Our Lady's Chapel, Balcarry, third field on right.

The English word 'fey' means strange or other-worldly. In Scotland it can describe a person fated to die soon. In Galloway the word has been used to describe a croft or a piece of infield land.

In one or two places in the Rhins area the word fey occurs in the title. An example of this is Chapel Fey, which lies about 600 metres north-north-west of Balcarry, near the mouth of the Water of Luce.

Chapel Fey is the site of a burial-ground and an associated chapel, which is said to have been dedicated to Our Lady (D, 58). Scott (Y, II, 347) records the historical existence of St Mary's chapel within Glenluce parish.

'In Balcarrie,' McKerlie states (H, II, 230), 'we have the Gaelic words *Baile* and *Carraig*, meaning the town or village, and a rock.' So, in earlier times Balcarry may have been a hamlet, giving more reason for finding a chapel in the vicinity.

A farm track presently leads from the Glenluce-Stair Haven road up to the site of the chapel and burial-ground. No remains of these are now visible, but their location is on the north side of the farm track.

In 1899, Rev George Wilson of Glenluce recorded the discovery, in the burial-ground, of a rosary and two amber beads. The latter are now in the National Museum of Antiquities, in Edinburgh. He also personally recollected the walls of Our Lady's Chapel, Balcarry, standing two or three feet high (E, 129).

According to McKerlie, (H, I, 173) the chapel at Balcarry belonged to the monks of Glenluce Abbey. It may have been an earlier established chapel, taken over by the monks; alternatively it could have been built by them, some time after the monastery's foundation in *c*. 1192. Before the Reformation in the 16th century all of this land was under the jurisdiction of Glenluce Abbey.

Our Lady's Chapel, near Balcarry, is one of a cluster of three or four chapels in this locality, the others being KirkChrist, St John's at Knock of Luce, and possibly Kilfillan.

There is evidence from remaining disjointed farm-track remnants that an old road once led from Corsehead, through Balcarry and Kilfillan to Milton. This medieval farm road was west of and linked to the then main road route from Glenluce to Whithorn, which passed through Corsehead and Milton (KirkChrist).

Access: *OS Map Ref NX 1997 5606*

The field site can be reached on foot from the farm track, which leads up through NO. 1 Balcarry steading, to the east of the road going south from Glenluce to Stair Haven. (See earlier section on St John's Chapel, Knock of Luce, for map.)

St Fillan's Chapel, Kilfillan

Kilfillan, presently, is a farm between Glenluce and Stair Haven, near the point where the River Luce flows into Luce Bay. During the Middle Ages in this area there were two pre-Reformation chapels, namely KirkChrist, to the east, and the other dedicated to Our Lady, at Balcarry, just to the north of Kilfillan.

McKerlie (H, II, 226-7) says:

> At Kilfillan the supposition is that a chapel at some time or other was there dedicated to St Fillan. There is, however, no trace of such a place of worship, and it seems to us rather close to KirkChrist.

Scott (Y, II, 347), without any substantiation, simply records the historical existence of St Fillan's Chapel at Kilfillan. No evidence or trace of this chapel remains today. Only the tradition of the name of the farm provides any credence for the chapel's existence. MacQueen (Q2, 19) says that the Airyolland Moss and farm-steadings, north of Glenwhan Moor and also in Old Luce parish, are from the Gaelic *airigh Fhaolain*, 'Faolan's sheiling', and indicate lands which formerly belonged to the church.

St Fillan (also known as Foellan or Foilan) was a native of Ireland who accompanied his mother, St Kentigerna, and his kinsman, St Comgan, to Scotland in the 8th century. He became a missionary monk in Scotland, and the place where he died is now called Strathfillan, which is the valley of the River Fillan between Crianlarich and Tyndrum, in Perthshire. There is a chapel in that area dedicated to the saint. King Robert the Bruce (1274-1329) adopted St Fillan as his patron saint.

From the end of the 12th century until around the time of the Reformation, Kilfillan and all the surrounding land belonged to the Cistercian monks of Glenluce Abbey. There may have been a chapel here before the monks arrived. If so, it would seem that the other two chapels of KirkChrist and Our Lady, which served the monks and local people, survived longer.

Access: *OS Map Ref NX 205 547*

Kilfillan Farm is eastwards of the Glenluce to Stair Haven road. (See earlier section on St John's Chapel, Knock of Luce, for map.)

Kilfeddar

Kilfeddar is a farmhouse, situated some 4.0 kilometres north of New Luce village and about 0.7 kilometre east of the Main Water of Luce. Its situation 10.0 kilometres northwards from Glenluce Abbey, coupled with its name, suggests that in medieval times the monks from the abbey may have built a chapel at this site. This would date the chapel's erection to between the 13th and 15th centuries.

McKerlie (s, 51) says:

> Kilfedder, not far from New Luce, on the east, where there is a cairn thus called, is supposed to indicate the site of a church once dedicated to St Peter, Prince of the Apostles — in the Gaelic form, *Cill Phetir*, or *Pheadair*.

There are no available records, nor is there any physical evidence of such a chapel. The retention of the name alone carries the traditional suggestion of the chapel's existence. But this farm at Kilfeddar certainly belonged to Glenluce Abbey. Its name is included in a feu charter list of abbey properties, transferred by the last abbot, Thomas Hay, to Gilbert, Earl of Cassillis, on 17 April 1572. (*Registrum Magni Sigilli* 1546/80-2202).

'The Deil's Dyke, a vast rampart through Galloway and Nithsdale, passes through Kilfedder.' (L, 232)

Another similar chapel site at Kilmacfadzean lies eastwards, 5.0 kilometres from Kilfeddar.

Access: *OS Map Ref NX 1535 6835*

By car, 5.0 kilometres north-eastwards from New Luce village to the bridge across the Main Water of Luce, near Pularyan. Then, cross-country on foot for 0.9 kilometre in an east-south-easterly direction to reach Kilfeddar.

Alternatively, 2.0 kilometres northwards from New Luce village to Stair Lodge. A farm-track then leads westwards and north-westwards for 3.0 kilometres to Kilfeddar.

Kilmacfadzean

The farmhouse of Kilmacfadzean lies 5.0 kilometres north-eastwards of New Luce village. According to MacQueen (Q2, 20) the Gaelic-derived name Kilmacfadzean means 'my little Patrick's church'. It is thought that in the medieval period, when the Cistercian monks of Glenluce Abbey farmed or managed so much of the surrounding land area, among the chapels they built was one at Kilmacfadzean. No written records are available nor does physical evidence provide corroboration; the name alone persists to give credence to the existence of the chapel. But this farm at Kilmacfadzean certainly belonged to Glenluce Abbey. Its name is included in a feu charter list of abbey properties, transferred by the last abbot, Thomas Hay, to Gilbert, Earl of Cassillis, on 17 April 1572. (*Registrum Magni Sigilli* 1546/80-2202).

In this northern moorland part of the Glenluce area, some 5.0 kilometres westwards of Kilmacfadzean, lies Kilfeddar, a farmhouse site similarly associated with a chapel.

Both chapels, at Kilmacfadzean and Kilfeddar, would have been erected probably between the 13th and 15th centuries.

Access: *OS Map Ref NX 2035 6750*

Travel by road 4.0 kilometres (2.5 miles) from New Luce village north-eastwards to Balmurrie Farm, then continue on the farm-track northwards a further 1.0 kilometre (0.6 mile) to reach Kilmacfadzean.

Kilgallioch

Kilgallioch is a remote, rock-strewn location in the moorland-forest area, about 10.5 kilometres (6.5 miles) north-east of New Luce village. Presently, in the locality, the name is pronounced Kilgallick. It is variously spelled Kilgallioch and Killgallioch. In the Pont-Blaeu map of 1654 it is named Kilgaillack.

As to the derivation of the name, it is generally considered to be from the Gaelic. McKerlie (H, II, 228) says that the prefix is probably 'from the Gaelic *coile*, for a wood, with Gill, from the Norse *gil*, a deep narrow glen or ravine with a burn at the bottom, and the Gaelic *loch* for a sheet of water.' The difficulty with this interpretation is that it does not adequately represent the reality of the location. Writing in 1877, the same author states, 'There is also an old burial ground at Killgallioch farm-house, where a chapel must have stood.' (ibid, 249). This now ruinous farm-house is in fact almost 0.5 kilometre to the south of the chapel and burial-ground site. Records at the Royal Commission on the Ancient and Historical Monuments of Scotland state, 'The name Kilgallioch is said to be a corruption of *Gill (Cill) na Cailleach* — the Nun's Chapel.' In this case, no nuns are on record at this location. The singular title may imply that this was originally the chapel of a lady recluse, a lady hermit; but this is highly conjectural and only has a basis in the assumed derivation of the place-name. Another McKerlie (s, 50) states that Kilgallioch is said (by Sir Herbert Maxwell) to mean the chapel as of the standing-stones. This intepretation has more substance for two reasons: it fits in with the more likely Gaelic derivation of the place-name and, secondly, the ancient Laggangairn Standing Stones' site is only about 1.0 kilometre distant to the south-west. Kilgallioch is therefore most likely to be a compound of four Gaelic words, which are aptly descriptive: *cill*, a cell, church, churchyard or burying ground; *ag*, at; *ail*, a stone or rock; *ach*, a field. Thus *cill-ag-ail-ach* becomes corrupted to Kilgallioch. This could either describe the proximity of the Standing Stones to the chapel, or, alternatively, it could even describe the actual rock-strewn, sloping field site of the chapel remains at Kilgallioch. Instead of the last syllable being derived from the Gaelic *ach* it may be derived from *iochd*, which means mercy, clemency, kindness, humanity, generosity or compassion. Since the derivation can only be conjectured, this allows for other possibilities, perhaps even the name of a saint to whom the chapel was dedicated — but no known saint's name readily fits in with the name Kilgallioch. It is interesting to note here the mixed tradition in the naming of the very earliest churches in the Rhins and the neighbouring Machars area of Galloway. The first stone church, erected at Whithorn in *c.* 397 by St Ninian, was dedicated to St Martin of Tours, but was popularly referred to as *Candida Casa*, the White House. Kirkmadrine Church, in the Rhins, probably dates from the 5th century and has retained the corrupted dedication name of St Martin. Clayshant, probably the next oldest church in the Rhins and not too distant in date from Kirkmadrine, has a corrupted Gaelic title meaning Holy Stone. Interpreting Kilgallioch from its Gaelic roots and finding its name associated with nearby very ancient stones is quite compatible with the naming practice associated with those other early churches. This may even support the very early date of origin of the chapel at Kilgallioch.

At this remote site on the route of the Southern Upland Way there are the ruins of a chapel, three wells, an old burial-ground and a complex of old sheep pens.

The chapel that stood at Kilgallioch would seem to have served two purposes: a wayside chapel for pilgrims through the early and medieval centuries as they journeyed by this route to and from Whithorn; and as a chapel-of-ease for the small scattered community of this remote, upland, country area. The interior dimensions of the chapel appear to be about 7 metres by 4 metres, the longitudinal axis being in an east-north-east to west-south-west direction, and with an entrance on the south-easterly wall. Strewn remaining stones still provide some evidence of the size, shape and location of the chapel. Although the chapel site is on a section of dry ground, immediately to the north and west there is a semi-dry water course, the result of seepage from the three nearby springs, the Wells of the Rees. In the 1972 survey carried out by staff members of the Royal Commission on the Ancient and Historical Monuments of Scotland the outline of a further walled structure was found some 16 metres south of the chapel.

About 25 metres west of the chapel remains there is an open, somewhat circular, low-mounded area, about 30 metres in diameter. This is recorded as a graveyard. There is no superficial evidence of graves and no gravestones.

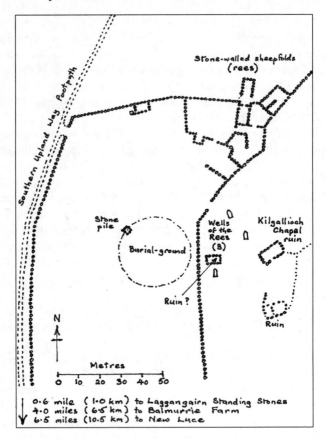

In the area between the chapel and the graveyard there are the three wells, known as the Wells of the Rees. The rees are a complex of sheep pens, composed of dry-stone walls, lying some 25 metres north of the chapel ruin. These rees may contain stones taken from the chapel. The Wells of the Rees are so named because of their proximity to these sheep rees. The wells are three springs, which are covered by domed structures of large unmortared stones, these being about 0.9 metre high with square openings at ground level, and above each lintel a recess, measuring 0.35 metre square and equally deep. The best preserved of the three is oblong, about 1.8 metres long and 1.2 metres broad. These wells would have some association with the chapel in former times, but their exact purpose is unclear. McKerlie (s, 53) remarks that these wells are reminiscent of South

Wales and the neighbourhood of St David's where similar ones are to be found.

This Kilgallioch chapel site is reached on foot cross-country. Centuries ago it was on one of the routes used by pilgrims on their way to and from Whithorn, to visit the shrine of St Ninian. It would be a welcome stopping place, before travelling on southwards to Glenluce Abbey and then on to Whithorn.

There is remaining evidence in the steading ruins at Laggangairn (also found spelled as Laggangarn), about 1.4 kilometres south-westwards from the ruins of Kilgallioch Chapel, that people lived in this remote area. It would seem that from the 5th or 6th century there were Christians in the area. Christian symbols engraved on the nearby Laggangairn Stones provide some evidence of this.

About 0.4 kilometre north of the ruined Laggangairn steadings, in a wide clearing, there are two standing stones. They are estimated to have been erected about 4,000 years ago. The details, including the reason, are lost in antiquity. This area of Galloway is rich in remains of those ancient times, including other standing stones, some stone circles, chambered cairns, and a multiplicity of stone cairns. Many of the latter may date into the period of Christian history and:

> have been raised by pilgrims from the north and west on their journey to St Ninian's relics at Whithorn. It was customary for pilgrims to add stones to such piles as they passed on their way. (H, II, 241)

McKerlie (ibid, 243) states that the standing stones at Laggangairn numbered thirteen at the end of the 18th century, but by 1877 there remained only seven. Today only two remain, and are under the care of Historic Scotland. The latter body says that there may originally have been fourteen stones. Evidence from McKerlie suggests that all the standing stones were incised with Christian crosses.

Both of the two remaining stones at Laggangairn have incised Latin crosses, each with four smaller crosses in the angles. These crosses are on the western outward face of both stones, which stand beside each other, about 0.6 metre apart. The larger, northerly stone stands 1.88 metres above ground level, while the other stone is 1.57 metres high; both are 0.66 metre broad. They are of grey, Silurian sandstone. In a descriptive plaque placed at the site by Historic Scotland it says:

> Christian memorials were added to these stones a little over 1,000 years ago by pilgrims on their way from the West of Scotland to the Shrine of St Ninian, at Whithorn.

Laggangairn Standing Stones

A similarly inscribed stone found at Drummore, in the Rhins, and now in the National Museum of Antiquities of Scotland (IB 33) has been dated to about the 6th-7th century. 'The reduplication of crosses on each stone, which is an indication of very early date, occurs at Bryngwyn, Radnorshire and elsewhere.' (E, 101) So, it may be that the Laggangairn Stones were inscribed with crosses as early as the 6th-7th century.

There are records of the removed stones from Laggangairn being used as lintels and doorposts. McKerlie (H, II, 243), writes in 1877:

> The site [Laggangairn] is about one hundred yards east from the farm-house, which was benefited by the use of some of the stones as lintels, also as gate posts. The new farm-house has three of the stones. At Killgallioch and Pultadie farm-houses there are two at each as gate-posts. One has been honoured by being built into the front of a new shed at Pultadie, on which there is a sculptured cross, formed of deep grooved lines, &c. They are all similarly sculptured, and evidently very ancient.

Kilgallioch and Laggangairn speak to us out of the silence of their stones and tell us about Christian life and influence, even in this remote part of Galloway, stretching over a period of some fourteen centuries. McKerlie (S, 51) speaking of Laggangairn says:

> Those stones were probably Druidic; and it is easy to recall the menhirs of Brittany, also turned into monuments of the Faith by sculptured

crucifixions, or surmounted by stone crosses. These stones and the curious wells across the Tarff (Tarf) constitute a most interesting cluster of venerable memorials, impregnated with the piety of early Catholic days, when what had been associated with a pagan cult was sanctified for Christian use.

Access:

OS Map Refs	*Kilgallioch Chapel*	*NX 2299 7232*
	Kilgallioch Burial-ground	*NX 2296 7231*
	Wells of the Rees	*NX 2298 7232*
	Laggangairn Standing Stones	*NX 2223 7166*
	Laggangairn Farm Ruin	*NX 2204 7141*

There is a fair measure of difficulty in reaching these sites.

Although other ways may be possible, an ordinary route would be to travel, preferably by car, from New Luce village by the Cross Water of Luce road, which links up with the Southern Upland Way, to the end of the surfaced road at Balmurrie Farm. This is a distance of 4.0 kilometres (2.5 miles). From there travel on foot in a north-easterly direction, following the route of the Southern Upland Way. After about 2.0 kilometres (1.25 miles) the forest area is reached. Southern Upland Way signs direct one along rough paths and Forestry Commission lane, via the Purgatory Burn, to Laggangairn farm ruins, where there is a bothy shelter, on a short distance to the Standing Stones, then over a footbridge crossing the Tarf Water, and on up the slightly ascending woodland footpath to the site of Kilgallioch Chapel ruins, its burial-ground, and the Wells of the Rees — indicated by a direction sign. The distance from Balmurrie Farm to Kilgallioch Chapel/Wells of the Rees is about 6.5 kilometres (4.0 miles). Walking this route can take at least two hours. It is a journey for the fit and healthy. Cross-country clothing and footwear are called for. Though it is an arduous and challenging journey, it has its rewards in the scenic beauty of the countryside and the interest of the sites visited.

Reflection

In this south-western part of Scotland, within the Rhins area and its adjacent part of West Wigtownshire, forty-two religious centres have been investigated whose foundations date between the 5th and 16th centuries. These forty-four religious sites include two abbeys, one early monastery, eight parish churches and thirty-three chapels.

Evidence in the form of building remains, sculptured artefacts, charter references, identification in maps, historical records, reports, letters, articles and books, as well as reported and recorded tradition, including analysis of place names, have all contributed in varying degrees to establish authenticity.

Of the forty-four religious sites, substantial or sufficient verification is available for thirty-seven of them.

Table 1. *Thirty-seven Authenticated Religious Sites*

Religious Houses	Parish Churches	Chapels
Soulseat Abbey	Kirkmadrine	St Medana's Cave
Glenluce Abbey	Kirkmaiden	St Medran's, Cardryne
	Clayshant	St Mary's, Maryport
	Inch	St Laisren's, Kirkleish, Inshanks
	Stoneykirk	Kildonan, near Drummore
	Kirkcolm	St Eochod's, Hallyholm/Kilstay
	Leswalt	St Bride's, Kirkbride, South Rhins
	Glenluce	St Finian's, Killingeane
		Kirkholm
		Chapel Rossan
		Kirkmabreck
		Kirkmagill
		Chapel of St John, Stranraer
		Chapel Patrick, Portpatrick
		St Ninian's, Killantringan
		St Catherine's, Eldrickhill
		Kildonan, near Drummore
		St Mary's, Kilmorie
		Killiecuddican
		Chapel Donnan, Balsarroch
		St Bride's, East Kirkbryde, North Rhins
		St John's, Knock of Luce
		KirkChrist, Milton
		Our Lady's, Balcarry
		Kilfeddar
		Kilmacfadzean
		Kilgallioch

Seven of the forty-four religious sites studied are of questionable validity. Sometimes only the name survives to provide any evidence.

Table 2. Seven Religious Sites of Questionable Validity

St Buite's Monastery, Dunman
St Ninian's Chapel, Chipperdingan
Killaser Chapel
Kirklauchline Chapel
Topmalloch Chapel
Cairnhapple Chapel
St Fillan's Chapel, Kilfillan

In this south-west area of Scotland, MacQueen (Q2, 24-26) assesses that more than three-quarters of all ancient church commemorations are of Celtic origin. He adds that the commemorations are predominantly Dark Age and Irish.

In the matter of church dedications, Butler (J, IV, 300) reminds us:

that all churches and ecclesiastical buildings are dedicated to God and to God only. Other names by which they may be known are those of saints or mysteries of religion in whose honour or under whose patronage they are dedicated. Nevertheless, custom allows the loose expression 'dedicated to such-and-such a saint'.

The titles we find for the centuries-old churches and chapels in the Rhins area express a familial spirituality, embracing Jesus, Mary and saints representative of Christendom.

Table 3 presents a list of all the accepted pre-Reformation Christian sites within the Rhins and its associated West-Wigtownshire area, together with some indication of the date of foundation of each religious centre.

In Table 3, the width of the band of centuries indicates the precision or imprecision of the date of each foundation: for some, the exact century is known; for others, the estimated date of foundation may range over a period of from two to eight centuries. The chart indicates only the date of foundation, not the period during which each church was in use.

The thirty-seven authenticated religious centres spread over a thousand years, from the 5th to the 15th century, provide some evidence of the extent and nature of Christian life in the Rhins area of Galloway during the early and medieval period. At that time, before the Reformation in 1560, all of this Christian life and worship was Catholic. As such, it had been instituted in an organised form by St Ninian, starting about the year 397. Through those early and

Table 3. Pre-Reformation Church Sites in the Rhins Area of Galloway

Abbey	Parish Church	Chapel	Title	Century of Foundation Actual or Estimated															
				1	2	3	4	5	6	7	8	9	10	11	12	13	14	15	16
		✖	St John's, Stranraer															■	■
		✖	Kilmacfadzean														■	■	
		✖	Kilfeddar														■	■	
		✖	St Mary's, Maryport														■	■	
		✖	St Catherine's, Eldrickhill													■	■		
	✖		Stoneykirk													■	■		
✖			Glenluce Abbey												■	■			
✖	✖		Soulseat Abbey												■	■			
		✖	Kirkholm											■	■	■			
		✖	Killiecuddican											■	■				
	✖		Kirkmaiden											■	■				
	✖		Glenluce										■	■					
	✖		Inch									■	■	■					
		✖	St Medana's Cave & Chapel								■	■	■	■	■	■	■	■	■
		✖	St John's, Knock of Luce								■	■	■	■	■	■	■		
		✖	Our Lady's, Balcarry								■	■	■	■	■	■			
		✖	KirkChrist, Milton								■	■	■	■	■	■			
		✖	St Bride's, Kirkbride								■	■	■	■	■	■			
		✖	St Ninian's, Killantringan								■	■	■	■	■	■	■		
		✖	St Laisren's, Kirkleish								■	■	■	■	■	■			
		✖	Kildonan, near Stoneykirk								■	■	■	■	■	■			
		✖	Kirkmagill								■	■	■	■	■	■			
		✖	Kirkmabreck								■	■	■	■	■	■			
		✖	St Eochod's, Hallyholm/Kilstay								■	■	■	■	■	■			
	✖		Leswalt							■	■	■	■	■	■	■			
		✖	St Bride's, East Kirkbryde								■	■	■	■	■	■			
		✖	Chapel Donnan, Balsarroch							■	■	■	■	■	■	■			
		✖	Chapel Patrick, Portpatrick							■	■	■	■	■	■	■			
		✖	Chapel Rossan							■	■	■	■	■	■	■			
		✖	Kildonan, near Drummore							■	■	■	■	■	■	■			
		✖	St Medran's, Cardryne							■	■	■	■	■	■	■			
		✖	St Mary's, Kilmorie							■	■	■	■	■	■	■			
	✖		Kirkcolm							■	■	■	■	■	■	■			
		✖	Kilgallioch						■	■	■	■	■	■	■	■	■		
		✖	St Finian's, Killingeane						■	■	■	■	■	■	■	■			
	✖		Clayshant					■	■										
	✖		Kirkmadrine					■	■	■	■	■	■	■	■	■			
				1	2	3	4	5	6	7	8	9	10	11	12	13	14	15	16

medieval centuries, the Mass — the Euchaistic Sacrifice, given to the apostolic Church by Our Lord at the Last Supper, with the injunction, 'Do this in commemoration of me' — was the central act of worship. Ordained priests, diocesan and religious, celebrated this Holy Sacrifice with the participation of the people. Attendance was obligatory on Sundays and on a few feastdays, but where there were regular priests daily Mass would be celebrated. The Creed, the Church's traditional profession of Faith, would be shared. In the Mass, too, Holy Scripture would be read and explained. It is recognised that despite the weakness of human nature, holiness is continuously evident in Christ's Church, and so, even though in pre-Reformation times the education level of the clergy was more disparate than at present, evangelising took place, people were exhorted and encouraged, sacraments were administered. The Church grew. It covered the country. It was evident. It was a central part of life experience, an integral part of the development and history of the country.

The fusion of the secular and the sacred, through the means of sanctification provided by Our Lord and given to his Church as its apostolic mission, can be recognised in history. That progress in sanctification, because it is of Christ, has assurance of attainment, but, because it involves humanity, carries with it the flaws of human weakness. History is littered with examples. History is the inter-mingling of the lives of sinners and saints. Despite human vicissitudes, holiness survives. The life of Christ in Christianity is a continuation of his loving sacrifice on Calvary. His strength overcomes human weakness. His holiness overcomes sin. His pain and suffering and love heal, restore and strengthen the brokenness of humanity. His Resurrection from the dead raises humanity to a life of fullness of grace. If we live with him in this life, then we ascend with him to share his eternal glory in heaven. There is faith and hope in Christianity, but it is founded on love. Christian history is a witness to this. Alas, it is also a witness to human folly and our need and dependence on God's love.

Here in the Rhins, we have a treasure chest of the history of the Church and its absorption into the life of the community through the centuries. Despite some valid criticism, the evidence is of an early and medieval Catholic Church integrated in the history and life of the people, providing the nourishment and encouragement and upbuilding of spiritual life, a life in compliance with Christ, a life with Christ as its essence and reality.

All of this may be sensed when visiting these ancient centres of Christianity. One is tangibly connected with the past, while being part of present experience, and feeling part of the mainstream of Christian life flowing into the future. In these various settings one can grow more aware of the wholeness of this Christian reality. There is a God-given naturalness to enjoy, a Christian history to be remembered, absorbed and appreciated, and an opportunity to glimpse the future. There is a unity, a peace, a meaning, an experience of an all-embracing reality, a sense of the Emmanuel, the-God-who-is-with-us, helping us, providing for us, seeking, inspiring and guiding us, sharing with us his goodness. In a special way, human history walks with God in these places.

There is a treasury of memories, and more to be treasured. The site of a carpet of snowdrops in the peace of old Inch churchyard on a sunlit, February morning. The glory of July's ox-eye daisies in the vicinity of Kirkbryde in the northern Rhins. The walk through a lush, summer meadow at Lady Well, near the site of the ancient KirkChrist Chapel. The sentinel, autumn grass of Kilbuie Moss, leading to the awesome precipitousness of the cliffs at Dunman. The rewards of the arduous trek to Kilgallioch.

In a personal way, I remember drawing at Eldrickhill and being surrounded by inquisitive calves. Drawing, too, from the chill of a December seat at Portpatrick and being absorbed by the peace and interest of the scene. The exhilaration of finding St Medana's Cave, after several unsuccessful attempts. Seeing fox and deer, and all the farm animals, bounding hare and suspicious rabbits. Experiencing the occasional annoyance of the flies, but filled with wonderment at the profusion of insect life. Delighting in nature's aviary. Enjoying the richness of such varied scenery. Sensing the presence of so many people of the past in the peace of the old churchyards and burial places. The meeting and conversation with so many kindly and diverse good people in country and town. The joy of discovery, the fruit of labour, the richness of experience, even transient disappointments and failures. All of these contribute to the total exhilaration and happiness obtained questing for heritage. That quest is rewarding. It is unifying and inspiring. It brings the present into contact with the past. It helps to explain the present. It provides a tangible continuum that points onwards to the future.

I realise that focusing on this single area of the Rhins of Galloway provides but a glimpse; nevertheless this glimpse of our total heritage is valuable in itself and, at the same time, illustrates a reality of which it is a worthy microcosm.

The thirty-seven definite Catholic centres — abbeys, parish churches and chapels — of pre-Reformation Christian history in the Rhins area compare with approximately the same number of present-day Christian denominational places of worship, including meeting halls, chapels and churches. Although the number of places of Christian worship has remained about the same, the population of the area has greatly increased from the medieval period up to the present day.

The Catholic parish of St Joseph, in Stranraer, celebrated its 150th anniversary as a parish in 1996. It is the only present-day Catholic parish church in the Rhins and neighbouring area. It is a link with the Catholic past. But it contrasts by its singleness with the thirty-seven Catholic centres of worship in existence in the same area before 1560, the time of the Reformation in Scotland.

Of the thirty-seven pre-Reformation Christian centres in the Rhins (with a further seven unvalidated centres) there are only two of them at present under government care, *viz.*, Glenluce Abbey and Kirkmadrine, both of which are in the care of Historic Scotland. Either at the national or local level, so much more is required for the preservation and maintenance of these precious heritage sites in the Rhins area. Some of them are so hidden, they are almost unknown. Neglect has taken its toll. Out of respect for the richness of this heritage, so much more needs to be done. This present study may hopefully contribute awareness and knowledge, and help generate appreciation and concern.

This study of historical places of Christianity in the Rhins area of Galloway shows, by their growth in number and foundational dates, which go back to the earliest period of Christian life in this country, that the area is outstanding for its concentration and expression of Church life through the centuries.

McKerlie (H, II, 164), writing in 1877, says:

> We think the assertion may be made with safety, that no other part of Scotland, in ancient times, could have surpassed Galloway for the number of ancient ecclesiastical buildings, large and small.

Organised Church life has been an integral part of community experience and history in Galloway since St Ninian's institution of his see of *Candida Casa* in AD *c.* 397. It continued in this Catholic tradition, with a fusion of Celtic and Roman spirituality and ordering, up to the mid-16th century. From that Reformation period the main texture of Christianity has been of the Scottish reformed Church tradition. Through the period of the past two centuries, Catholic life has been allowed to re-enter and take its restored place alongside the predominant Protestantism. There is a spirit of accommodation, acceptance and co-operation. There is a mutual respect for these distinctive expressions of the Christian Faith. Although there is a general acceptance of the right to choose freely and practise, with integrity, a particular expression of Christian faith and life, nevertheless there remains the related issue of the unity of Christianity. All Christians are united in Christ. This unity is real in the mystical sense, but presently there is a fragmentary incompleteness in the areas of structure, doctrine, government and sacramental intercommunion. Our Lord prayed his Eucharistic prayer at the last Supper, 'May they all be one, Father, may they be one in us, as you are in me and I am in you.' (John 17:21). He has given us this as our Christian prayer. We pray for its realisation. We pray in hope and faith and love. We look for the achievement of our Christian unity according to the mind of Christ.

This book hopefully will provide some contribution to that end by highlighting the rich, long, tested tradition of our shared Christian heritage. Despite pagan ravages and the inevitable difficulties of assimilating a succession of diverse cultural influences, social structures and religious differences, Christianity has flourished in this area for sixteen centuries. Appreciating and sharing this together can contribute to a unity of purpose, not only to cherish mutually this common legacy but to be inspired to pass this heritage on as best we can to the generations to come. That will be a blessed enterprise. In Christ there is a unity of past, present and future. In our unity in Christ may we greatly treasure our common Christian heritage, be inspired by what it communicates to us, make our living contribution to it, and present it as a life-giving Faith to those yet to come.

References

A   *The Parishes of Medieval Scotland,* by Ian B Cowan (1967). Scottish Record Society Vol 93, Edinburgh.

B   *Medieval Religious Houses — Scotland,* by Ian B Cowan & David E Easson, 2nd Edn (1976). Longmans, London.

C   'The Archaeological Sites and Monuments of Scotland', No. 24, West Rhins, Wigtown District, Dumfries & Galloway Region, by Royal Commission on the Ancient Historical Monuments of Scotland (1985).

D   'The Archaeological Sites and Monuments of Scotland', No. 26, East Rhins, Wigtown District, Dumfries & Galloway Region, by Royal Commission on the Ancient Historical Monuments of Scotland (1987).

E   Fourth Report and Inventory of Monuments and Constructions in Galloway', Vol 1, County of Wigtown, by Royal Commission on the Ancient and Historical Monuments and Constructions of Scotland (1912). HMSO.

F   *The Parish History of Kirkmaiden,* by William Todd, written in 1854 in his 80th year, having been schoolmaster in the parish for 47 years. Published, in his handwriting, by Galloway Collection.

G   *A Large Description of Galloway,* written in 1684 by Andrew Symson. W & C Tait, Edinburgh (1823).

H   *History of the Lands and Their Owners in Galloway,* Vols 1 & 2, by P H McKerlie, 1877. Published by G C Book Publishers Ltd (1995).

I   *The Book of Saints* by Benedictine Monks of St Augustine's Abbey, Ramsgate, 6th Edn (1994). Cassell, London.

J   *Butler's Lives of the Saints,* edited by H Thurston SJ & D Attwater, Vols 1 to 4 (1956). Burns & Oates.

K   *Wigtownshire Charters,* edited by R C Reid (1960). Scottish History Society, Edinburgh.

L   *New Statistical Account of Scotland — Wigtownshire* by Ministers of the Respective Parishes (1841). William Blackwood & Sons, Edinburgh.

M   *Caledonia,* Vols 1 & 5, by George Chalmers (1867).

N   *Dumfriesshire & Galloway Natural History & Antiquarian Society Transactions 1948-49,* Third Series Vol XVII (Whithorn Volume), edited by R C Reid (1950).

O   *Dumfriesshire & Galloway Natural History & Antiquarian Society Transactions 1951-52,* Third Series Vol XXX. Editors R C Reid & A E Truckell (1953).

P1   *From Christ to Constantine — the first three hundred years of the Church,* by Anthony Meredith SJ (1995). CTS Publications, London.

P2   *The Medieval Church — A Brief History,* by Joseph H Lynch (1994). Longman, London & New York.

Q1   Article 'In Obedience and Reverence: Whithorn and York *c.* 1128-*c.* 1250' by Richard D Oram in *The Innes Review* Vol XLII, No. 2, Autumn 1991.

Q2   Article 'The Gaelic Speakers of Galloway and Carrick' by J MacQueen in Scottish Studies Vol 17, ed. J MacQueen (1973). School of Scottish Studies, University of Edinburgh.

R   *The Imperial Gazetteer of Scotland* Vol II, edited by John Marius Wilson (undated *c.* 1854). A Fullarton & Co, London & Edinburgh.

S   *Pilgrim Spots in Galloway* by E Marianne & H McKerlie (1916). Sands & Co, London & Edinburgh.

T   *A Journey Through Time, 1.— The Christian Heritage of Wigtownshire.* Written by R D Oram for the Whithorn Trust & The Dumfries & Galloway Tourist. Board (undated)

U   *The Ecclesiastical Architecture of Scotland,* Vols I, II & III, by D MacGibbon & T Ross (1991). James Thin, The Mercat Press, Edinburgh

V   *History of the Parish and Abbey of Glenluce,* by J M Rusk (1930). Published Wm Blackwood & Sons Ltd, Edinburgh & London.

W   *The Hereditary Sheriffs of Galloway,* by Sir Andrew Agnew (1893). Vols 1 & 2. David Douglas, Edinburgh.

X   *Fasti Ecclesiae Scoticanae* by Hew Scott, Part 2 (1867). William Paterson, Edinburgh, & John Russell Smith, London.

Y   *Fasti Ecclesiae Scoticanae,* by Hew Scott, Vol 2 (1917) and Vol 8 (1950). Oliver & Boyd, Edinburgh: Tweeddale Court.

Z   *Scottish Parish Clergy at the Reformation 1540-1574,* by Charles H Haws (1972). Scottish Record Society, New Series 3, Edinburgh.

Select Bibliography

The Place Names of Galloway, by Sir Herbert Maxwell (1930). Jackson, Wylie & Co.

A Dictionary of Scottish Place Names, by Mike Darton (1990). Lochar Publishing, Moffat.

Hereditary Sheriffs of Galloway, by Sir Andrew Agnew, Vol 1, (1893). Douglas.

A History of Dumfries and Galloway, by Sir Herbert Maxwell (1896). William Blackwood & Sons, Edinburgh & London.

History of Galloway, Vol 1, by Rev William MacKenzie (1841). J Nicholson of Kirkcudbright.

A Journey Through Time 2 — The Archaeology of Wigtownshire, written by R D Oram for the Whithorn Trust and Dumfries & Galloway Tourist Board. With assistance from the Wigtown Rural Development Company (undated).

The Visitors' Guide to Wigtownshire, by William McIlwraith (1875). *Wigtown Free Press* Office, Stranraer.

The Statistical Account of Scotland 1791-1799, Vol v, Stewartry of Kirkcudbright and Wigtownshire, (1983) edited by Sir John Sinclair. EP Publishing Ltd, Wakefield.

Collins Encyclopaedia of Scotland, edited by John Keay & Julia Keay (1994). Harper Collins.

The Buildings of Scotland — Dumfries & Galloway, by John Gifford (1996). Penguin Books.

The Early Christian Monuments of Scotland, by J Romilly Allen (1903). Society of Antiquaries of Scotland, Edinburgh.

Portpatrick Through The Ages, by R R Cunningham (1974). Revised edn. 1993. *Wigtown Free Press*, Stranraer.

The Abbey of Glenluce, by the Department of the Environment (1974). HMSO, Scotland.

Glenluce Abbey, by Doreen Grove, edited by Chris Tabraham (1996). Historic Scotland.

A Note for Visitors to Soulseat, by Joanna Gordon (1989).

The Jerusalem Bible, (1968). Darton, Longman & Todd, London.

Monasticum Praemonstratense, Vol 2, by Norbert Backmund O Praem., Straubing (1952) Cl. Attenkofersche Buchdruckerei.

A Dictionary of the Popes, by Donald Attwater (1939). The Catholic Book Club, London.

The Catholic Directory for Scotland, by authority of the Archbishops and Bishops of Scotland (1996). John S Burns & Sons, Glasgow.

The Innes Review, Vol XL, No. 2, Autumn 1989 & Vol XLII No. 2, Autumn 1991. The Scottish Catholic Historical Association.

The Scottish Reformation, by Ian B Cowan (1982). Weidenfeld & Nicolson, London.

The New Cambridge Modern History II: The Reformation 1520-1559, edited by G R Elton (1965). Cambridge UP.

The New Cambridge Modern History III: The Counter Reformation & Price Revolution 1559-1610, edited by R B Wernham (1968). Cambridge UP.

Wild Men and Holy Places, by Daphne Brooke (1994). Canongate Press, Edinburgh.

Scottish Church History, by Gordon Donaldson (1985). Scottish Academic Press, Edinburgh.

Maps Consulted

Map of Galloway by Timothy Pont (1654), Johan Blaeu.

Map of Scotland by Robert Morden (1695 reproduction of 1687 original).

Maps of Wigtownshire, Sheets 1-4, by General William Roy (*c.* 1747).

Map of Wigtownshire by John Ainslie (1782).

Map of the County of Wigtown, Sheet 8, by William Johnson (1826).

Ordnance Survey Maps of Rhins, Sheets 1 & 3 (1856) Scale 1/63360.

Ordnance Survey Maps of Wigtownshire (1908) Scale 1/2500.

Ordnance Survey Map of Rhins, Sheet NX 06 (1959) Scale 1/25000.

Ordnance Survey Map of Stranraer, Glenluce & Surrounding Area, Sheet 82 Landranger Series (1986) Scale 1/50000.

Acknowledgements

To Staff of Public Library, Stranraer

Staff of Ewart Library, Dumfries

Roads Department, Stranraer (Dumfries & Galloway Council)

Scottish Catholic Archives, Edinburgh

Staff of Meadowsweet Herb Garden, Soulseat

Scottish Record Office, The National Archives of Scotland, Edinburgh

Royal Scottish Geographical Society, Glasgow

Map Library, National Library of Scotland, Edinburgh

Cistercian Monks of Sancta Maria Abbey, Nunraw

Premonstratensian Canons of Holy Trinity Abbey, Kilnacroft, Ballyjamesduff, County Cavan, Ireland

Central Catholic Library Association, Dublin, Ireland

John Donald Publishers Ltd, Edinburgh: Russell Walker, Commissioning Editor

Right Revd Maurice Taylor, Bishop of Galloway

Miss Helen Nelson

Staff of Glenluce Abbey

Historic Scotland, Edinburgh

Royal Commission on the Ancient and Historical Monuments of Scotland (National Monuments Record of Scotland), Edinburgh

Edinburgh City Council Central Library

Scotus College, Bearsden

and to the many individuals who gave me of their time, knowledge, interest and kindness.

Stranraer, 1997   *John McLean*